MW00777637

DO YOU STILL TALK TO GRANDMA?

DO YOU STILL TALK TO GRANDMA?

When the Problematic
People in Our Lives Are
the Ones We Love

BRIT BARRON

CONVERGENT

NEW YORK

Published in the United States by Convergent Books,
an imprint of Random House, a division of
Penguin Random House LLC, New York.

CONVERGENT BOOKS is a registered trademark and the Convergent
colophon is a trademark of Penguin Random House LLC.

Hardback ISBN: 978-0-593-59434-6
Ebook ISBN: 978-0-593-59435-3

Printed in the United States of America on acid-free paper

convergentbooks.com

2 4 6 8 9 7 5 3 1

First Edition

Book design by Susan Turner

For everyone who feels behind.
For everyone waiting for the people around them to catch up.
And for everyone in between.

CONTENTS

INTRODUCTION

I AM NOT THE ONLY PERSON WHOSE LIFE HAS PERMANENTLY changed since 2020. Actually, I don't know anyone whose life has stayed the same since that fateful year. Everything stopped, slowed down, and sped up all at the same time. In this country, a summer of revolution was upon us, and after months in our homes that gave us the space and time to ask questions and have conversations that had previously (and seemingly eternally) been on the back burner, many of our individual lives mirrored the chaos and trauma of our communal life. Beyond the agony of watching America, in all of its glory, disappoint me yet again, I had to face another profoundly disappointing and disorienting reality.

In 2020, my parents decided to get divorced. Somewhere around half of all marriages take this path—a fact,

I discovered, that doesn't make it one bit easier for the people involved. My parents had been married for thirty-eight years, and as someone who grew up in the church with my parents, I saw them as models of what successful marriage looked like. They had led small groups for young married couples, mentored younger couples, spoken at marriage retreats—there was never a time when I thought divorce would be a part of my reality. And yet here I was, thirty-five years old, four years into my own marriage, and navigating this imminent, permanent, and wildly disorienting change in my family.

There were and still are many layers for me to understand and unpack. I was incredibly close to my parents. I joked that they were my roommates when I moved in with them during grad school and then again after I got engaged and was saving money for my wedding. I often referred to them as my best friends. I told them everything. I talked to my mom on the phone nearly every day, and for seven straight years my dad and I got coffee on Friday mornings. I knew them, I knew my place in their world, I knew the safety and connection that I had—and then I knew nothing. I was rattled. My inmost self, the person they had formed and loved and nurtured together, was thrown into unrest. These people I knew and loved, these people whose relationship I wanted and envied, these people I thought would never change were now changing, they were moving. I watched them as they seemed to stand on opposing sides of an impassable chasm. They said things about each other that I wouldn't have believed they would ever say about anyone, let alone their husband or wife. It was as if my whole life I thought I was standing on solid ground, but I was actually standing on a spinning carnival ride that someone had finally switched on after thirty-five years. I was spinning and spinning, while the things I held close were ripped from my hands. I couldn't compete with the force of this sudden movement.

By the time I found my footing, when I was finally able to get off the spinning carnival ride and look around, nothing was the same. On the walls of my mind that once held family photos, there were now blank spaces. In my calendar, the spots once reserved for time with my best friends were now available, but what could possibly fill them? I struggled to know all that I was feeling, but one thing I knew clearly, what was loudest and most palpable, was disappointment. I felt that they had let me down as a couple and as individuals. I felt that I had let myself down by allowing myself to feel secure in something unreliable.

As a strong Enneagram type seven—the Enthusiast, the person who is extroverted and optimistic, and who avoids situations of pain and loss—disappointment was not a feeling I was super familiar with, not like this. I didn't know what to do with disappointment. Disappointment felt more personal and more intimate than anger. In retrospect, I understood why it hit so hard when my parents would tell me, "I'm not mad, I'm just disappointed." Well, the tables were now turned. But what was I to do with this massive disappointment that had to exist alongside massive love and care? I was disappointed, but I still loved them. I knew that they were and always would be my people, even while I also knew that things couldn't and wouldn't ever be the same.

I needed to learn how to live through a season of holding love and care and profound disappointment all at once. And I had no idea how to do that. I had more questions than answers, but over time (and with lots of help from my therapist), I knew a few things: I still wanted relationships with my parents, and I also needed space, needed to establish new boundaries, needed time to ask myself what the next season of my relationship with them could look like. So that's what I did. I set boundaries, I took space, and I dove more deeply into my trauma than I would have liked. This process gave me the space to think through some big questions that I would definitely face again:

What do I do when the people I love disappoint me?
What kinds of wrongs call for cutting someone off versus setting new boundaries?
What kind of apology is acceptable, and how do I forgive?
How quickly can I expect people to change and grow?
What do I have to let go of to be in relationships with people who hurt me?
Do I truly want to let those things go?

The beauty of this situation with my family was that it was private. We were in the middle of a pandemic, people weren't out and about, and my parents weren't regularly on social media, so we had privacy. I was processing this experience with my wife, my siblings, and my closest friends, and I didn't know what a gift that was until another disappointing experience not long after.

I met Rachel Hollis around 2014. We became friends long before either of us had any public professional success. Rachel and I had navigated all of the normal conversations that friends navigate. We met at the church where I was a pastor and where she and her family attended. This church was not accepting of queer people, and when I met Rachel, my wife and I (we weren't married yet) were both pretty deep in the closet, and we knew that if we came out, we would lose whatever community we had built there. Of course, we eventually concluded that love and truth were worth the cost of whatever losses we would suffer. We came out knowing that we would lose friends, our church home, our community, and our jobs. All of that was true, but along the way, some people surprised us. Rachel was one of those people. As soon as she found out about Sami (that's my wife) and me, she was on our side. When she found out that the church had rejected us, she and her family left that church, which was a socially and spiritually costly decision for them, so we had some solidarity. And it felt good for us to have friends on our side. Around a year after coming out and leaving the church, when we decided to get married, Rachel was at our wedding. We were with her through her time as a foster parent, and we have enjoyed many a happy hour together, gone on vacations, celebrated victories, put on events, and spent hours on phone calls and over drinks when her marriage was in trouble. We took a road trip to attend the funeral of our mutual best friend's mom. We have been the kind of friends who do what friends do: We have lived life together. And in 2019 that life got a little more complicated. Rachel wrote a book that skyrocketed her career and fame, and a lot of things changed. Her life, including our friendship, became public. Small events in a hotel conference room turned into stadium tours, and road trips to Santa Barbara turned into private planes to New York to meet Oprah.

Then in March 2021, Rachel shared a video on social media about not wanting to be relatable. Everything about the video was a big miss, and it was clear that she was not self-aware about the meaning of her social location as a privileged, now wealthy white woman in her thirties. The video generated an enormous controversy. I saw the video before the masses had found it, and I called her and was like, "Hey, what's up with this video? It looks like you're comparing yourself to Harriet Tubman and that's insane." We chatted only for a moment because she was at Six Flags with her boys, so I told her to call me later. Well, by the time she left the park, shit had already hit the fan. But apart from the public nature of the scandal, for me, the reality was that I was once again facing deep disappointment in someone I loved deeply. If my recent experience with my parents had taught me anything, it was that just because there was a deep love and relationship, that didn't mean the disappointment wasn't real. So how to hold that tension? What was the magical equation I could use to calculate my relationships? Well, it turns out there isn't one. I knew that as I

stomped my way through the murky waters of my relationship to my parents, and now here I was again, knee-deep in
murkiness with a friend. But unlike my private experience
with my parents' divorce, this disappointment also thrust
me into the company of thousands of strangers who all had
an opinion about what I was supposed to do.

I opened Instagram that night, and I had hundreds of
direct messages—I have no idea how many because the
notification just permanently said "99+" no matter how
many messages I opened. It was like playing a game of
Whac-A-Mole.

It was intense. Overwhelmingly, I was being pressured
to make a public statement saying that what Rachel did was
bad and, more specifically, that it was racist. "We need to
know where you stand." That's what a lot of people were
telling me, which was sort of funny. I thought, *You want to
know where I stand on what? On racism? I have literally spent a career
creating conversations and content around understanding racism and
developing an antiracist mindset.* I have tons of content read-
ily available on the Internet that would tell anyone who's
interested exactly where I stand on racism. What people
were demanding of me felt like something else—it felt as
if they were saying, "All of us are against this person now,
and if you don't join us, you are not radical enough." I even
had friends whom I hadn't spoken to since college text me
with questions like, "What do you think about your friend
Rachel?"

It was rude. And yet, what *was* I supposed to think of my
friend Rachel? Now, in addition to the questions I'd already

been working through because of my parents, about love and disappointment and change and expectations, I was being confronted by another pressing question:

> Do I have a responsibility to any of these strangers on the internet claiming to have all the right answers for me and demanding that I take action?

Of course I felt profoundly disappointed to see Rachel say and write what she did, but I was also not naïve enough to believe that white people in America who started an anti-racism journey in 2020 had become fully formed antiracists by 2021. There were two things that I felt confident in: I did not need to come to Rachel's rescue, and I did not need to throw her under the bus. Living with the whole truth often means living with two contradictory truths at the same time—love and disappointment, friendship and letdown, needing neither to save nor to condemn.

Rachel was my friend who had been there for me and who had also said something racist online. My parents were the best parents I could have asked for, and they also threw our family and my life into chaos. Could I hope that the strangers online could also learn to hold more than one truth at the same time?

I began to realize that we needed a new option, a new path to take.

Think of a recent failure by a celebrity or public figure. What happens after their failure, both with them and with us, follows a predictable path. We release the kraken on them, and the kraken, of course, takes the monstrous form of comments and messages, online think pieces, pressure applied to the people around them and to the people who do business with them to hold the guilty person accountable. Then we wait for a public apology, and they give us one, but it's still not enough. We unfollow them and wait for the next failure.

Now, don't get me wrong, there is a part of me that loves that there are real consequences for not being awake and aware of the world around you. I love that there is pressure to evolve and to grow. I love that accountability is assumed. What makes me nervous is that we have become too comfortable and confident interacting with people on the flat plane of the internet, and we have started to think that this is how relationships work.

I followed a woman on Instagram for years. I liked her content, she was funny, and she would post good recipes. Then she had two kids, and all of her content slowly became dominated by content about kids—and good for her. But as a person who has no kids and no plans to have kids, I lost interest, I unfollowed her, and I never looked back. That's just how the internet works. And that is one of its best qualities—it's not personal. It's a flat space that satisfies our deepest cravings for black and white, right and wrong, and it gives us almost instant gratification. Don't like something? Disappointed in someone? Bored? Click a button and it's gone. It's great . . . but it's not real.

I fear that we have taken our interactions from that flat space and followed the shortcut that the internet offers us around the hard relationship questions that are far, far more complicated than life online. I remember sitting around a table of friends when someone mentioned that their grandma voted for Trump, and after a loud gasp, someone else asked her, "Do you still talk to her?" She looked at that person with confusion, remained composed, and finally responded, "My nana? Yes, I still talk to her."

I understand what it feels like to draw this line in the sand. In fact, right after the 2020 election, I drew that same line.

These questions of what to do when the people we love—or just know, or just know about from public or online life—disappoint us are not new questions. Likewise, what accountability should look like and who gets to make that decision is not a new problem either. But the number of conversations we are involved in, the amount of information and input we have, and the degree to which we participate in people's public lives has grown exponentially with the advent of social media, and I believe we have reached a point in our culture that requires us to take a much more curious and careful look.

I love accountability. I love that there are real-life consequences for being racist. And I also wonder what comes next. Does accountability leave room for growth and change? Can we come back from making a mistake? Even if it was a racist one? What is the difference between consequences and punishments, and who is getting to decide these things?

This is the conversation that I want to have, not because

I have all the answers, but because I am looking around and I see that we need to be asking different questions. The people I love have disappointed me, and I have disappointed many people. I have worked through slow and confusing and complicated human relationships, and I have lived enough life to know that I haven't always had the right answers. There are lots of things I used to believe that make me cringe now; I have changed and evolved and grown. I was not born knowing everything I needed to know, and I still don't know it all now. So, how can we let all of that be true?

Our life is not flat, so we need to stop trying to draw straight lines over a topographical map. Life doesn't work that way, and this way of trying to manage life is not working for us.

We need mountains, peaks, and valleys; we need conversations; we need accountability that's more transformational than formulaic. We need to get back to being human, to allowing for nuance in our own lives and for nuance in the lives of the people around us. We need conversations, and we need not to be so quick to cut people from our lives. We need less standing on the right side of the line and more realizing it's not actually a line, but a complex web we have to navigate and tend together.

DO YOU STILL TALK TO GRANDMA?

1

Moving Beyond Heroes and Villains

I HAVE COMPLICATED FEELINGS ABOUT THE FAITH TRADI-
tion I grew up in. This faith was the home I lived in,
through which I understood the world for most of my
life, but now I find that most of the work I do involves
fighting systems, ideas, and practices that are entangled
with or arose from evangelical Christianity. I hit my ado-
lescence in the nineties. It was a wild time when you could
exist in a world within a world: You could live completely
in the evangelical bubble. You could attend a Christian
school, go to church, be a part of a youth group, join
a Christian sports league, watch Christian movies, wear
Christian clothing, listen to Christian music, shop at
Christian bookstores, and—yeah, it definitely sounds
like a cult. But that is the world I grew up in, and in that

world there were a lot of ideas about how life worked. Some were helpful; many were not.

I can still feel the deep pit in my stomach when I remember sitting in a youth room with a handful of other teenage girls while a man in his early twenties lectured us about the importance of virginity. That is the world I grew up in. Despite my discomfort, I lived much of my life in service to evangelicalism and to the world evangelicals created to sustain it. I attended an evangelical university and graduate school, and then I worked at a different evangelical university before becoming a pastor at an evangelical megachurch. I found a home and security in this world within a world, and I gave that home everything I had even though it was a home that was not safe for me, or secure. There were rules that we all had to follow to stay inside that home—rules I did not fit in, a fact that eventually resulted in an experience of painful spiritual loss. I gave my life to something only to be rejected by it once I became more of myself. My faith tradition, or rather the people who were using that tradition to gain power in the world, handed me trauma and heartache and years of confusion. For a while I just accepted that I could no longer be a part of this faith community and its way of understanding the world, and in some ways that was true: I did not fit in the evangelical world in the way it was being presented, in the way I had previously understood it. But was that the end?

I spent a lot of time wondering if there was still a way for me to keep my faith, to let go of the things that no longer served me but to cling even more tightly to the things

that did. Was there any good in Christianity? Could the
good still be valid amid all the bad? How could I separate
the two?

I quickly found myself navigating competing realities.
I found that I could not completely sort parts of my faith
heritage into one box or another, good or bad. The deeper
I dug, the more I found moments and experiences that represented more than one truth. For example, I realized that
I am still in financial debt to an evangelical university that I
wouldn't set foot in today, but this same university is also a
place that produced some of the deepest and truest friendships that I have in this world. I remember standing at my
wedding and looking around at the closest people in my
life standing beside me and realizing that all but one of
them came from that university. We all hated the place, but
that place we all hated brought us together. Growing up in
the church and having so many leadership opportunities
and chances to speak and preach was an experience like
no other, and as a person who now earns a living by speaking, I can see clearly that the thousands of hours that I got
to practice in this community made me the speaker that I
am today. And beyond practical skills, the church and my
faith gave me a sense of comfort and security in the world.
Believing that there is a God who is for me and loves me
is an incredibly helpful framework—and yet that the same
God was somehow obsessed with my virginity was weird.
What was I to do with these competing realities? Could
more than one thing be true at the same time? Could I
stand against the patriarchy, white supremacy, and general

nonsense of evangelicalism but also find wisdom and goodness in the Christian tradition? Can I grieve my time at
an evangelical university that gave me equal parts trauma
and financial debt while also deeply cherishing the friendships that I made there? I made it my mission to try to have
both, to hold both, to keep my faith, and to fight against the
abuse of power that caused me pain.

A few years after I began this journey, I had the extraor-
dinary privilege to spend a weekend with a man named
Richard Rohr. Rohr is a Franciscan priest who holds many
of the really progressive, cutting-edge ideas about faith that
a lot of us have now, but he came to them about thirty
years ago. Like me and many others, Rohr had gripes with
the powerful empire of evangelical Christianity, but he had
something I didn't have: information. Rohr had expert
knowledge of the wider (and older) Christian tradition and
all of the faithful people in that tradition who have discovered its wildly progressive and universal ancient wisdom.
He had explored all of the places I wanted to go, and he
left a map for all of the people who might want to follow
the same path. Well, I was one of those people, and Rohr
became a guide for me. I got to hang out with him for two
days—I was in spiritual nerd heaven.

There was a group of twenty of us, all people who had
big questions about faith, spirituality, and what it means to
be human, and who also had started faith lives in evangelicalism but had since left. We all had our own reasons why
we were on this journey of religious deconstruction, desperately following along and picking up the breadcrumbs

Father Rohr had left for us to find. Some of us left evangelicalism because of our own identity, some because of beliefs, others because of the corruption or collapse of a church. But one thing was very clear: We had all experienced loss. When we spoke that weekend and asked questions, several of us spoke with anger, sarcasm, and general disrespect for evangelicalism. We spoke in a tone that suggested that we believed we were better than them—those antiquated evangelicals. They were dumb and wrong, and we were the ones who crammed into this room with this man because we were the ones who were going to do it better—*be* better—because we were the ones who *were* better. I just knew Rohr felt the same.

Richard Rohr knew that all of the people who hurt us, who forced us out of their houses and into this room, were bad and wrong—right? We were only about one day into our time with him when he shut down that idea in me.

Someone asked a question, the kind of question that's a self-congratulatory comment in disguise, like "Why do you think it is that evangelicals are so interested in hoarding power for themselves and seemingly uninterested in the actual tradition and history of Christianity? Wouldn't it be more advantageous and truer to the tradition if they adopted a more universal lens and approach to ministry?" We all nodded our heads when it was asked, familiar with this opportunity to talk about how wrong the other team was. We waited for our new leader to lead the way, but he didn't. (Isn't it so interesting how we always seem to be looking for a new external authority? How did I go from "all

of those pastors are wrong" to "I only listen to Richard
Rohr now"? Or I've heard friends say things like "I'm done
with church," but then Brené Brown is very obviously their
pastor.)

Rohr paused and then told us all of the issues he saw
with the evangelical church, and all of our heads were
furiously nodding as he spoke about greed and power and
unwarranted exclusivity and so on. Then he said, "I'd like
to also take a moment and tell you a few things they have
taught me."

I was like, *What? No, you're the cool, progressive guy; you don't
get to say something good about the thing we all hate.* I was confused
and also maybe a little mad. *Why do you get to acknowledge
anything good?*

I sat with what he said, the critique and the praise, and
I wondered if the critique was enough to cancel out the
praise or vice versa. But why? Why couldn't I hold both
at the same time? This man had found a way out of the
binary and hard lines that I felt trapped in, and I desperately wanted that.

Most of us have been seduced into binary thinking—
not just evangelicals or Christians generally. It is everywhere
you look. In our storytelling, there are good people and bad
people. In our history, we have people on the right side
and wrong side. In our art, we have light and dark, and
as far as the eye can see, we are pushing ourselves and the
world around us into binary thinking. We are always trying
to make a world where there are heroes and villains, good
and evil, right and wrong, and where we can be the heroes,

where we can be good and right. People love categories and boxes and clean lines. We like it when the world is easy to understand. We want to know if a relationship is healthy or toxic. We want to know if someone is straight or gay, male or female. We want to know if our friends or family or partners are feeling happy or sad. We want to know if our careers are a success or a failure.

But the truth is more complex. Reality often comes in degrees, not binary poles. The world is not black and white, and neither are we. But that is complicated, that is hard, that is messy, and to be honest, that truth is not really as comforting. Perhaps the most enticing part of binary thinking is that it creates a world in which we could be right. We can eat, sleep, and breathe on the "right" side of the line, we can be continually and eternally good, we can have the right theology, the right ideology, the right parenting method, the right language, the right kind of activism, the right everything so that we will only ever land on the side of the hero and never the villain.

Our yearning for a simplistic, binary world of heroes and villains only becomes more intense online. All it takes to appease our craving to be on the side of right is to repost the right people. Social media has reinforced for us the belief that there is a right answer to everything, and not only that, but the right answer can also fit into just 240 characters. We reward people who have the "right" answers, and if someone doesn't know the right answer or perhaps believes the wrong thing, then *they* are wrong. It is simple. We have allowed it to become an all-or-nothing, the-more-you-lose-the-more-I-win, zero-sum game on the internet. But the problem is, real life is not a zero-sum game. Allowing ourselves to spend so much time in a space that feeds and feeds on the binary and the "certainty" parts of our brain has convinced some of us that life actually is that simple: "Someone says a bad thing; they are bad."

Our desire for, and tendency toward, binary thinking and polarization is actually a psychological phenomenon known as "splitting." Psychoanalyst Melanie Klein defined this form of psychic functioning—splitting the world into good or bad, friends or foes, "like" and "do not like"—as the "paranoid-schizoid position." This concept can help explain our tendency to consider differences not simply as variations but as opposites. More than that, it suggests how quickly our thinking can regress to a mode that is developmentally most appropriate for young children, who are incapable of dealing with ambivalence and complexity. According to Klein's psychoanalytic theory of "object relations," children split objects into all-good or all-bad—and they act accordingly—and this habit is an irrational yet helpful way of simplifying and managing reality. The coping mechanism that helped us navigate the world when we were young remains with us as adults.

We all tend to reject complexity. I think it is this tendency that is activated and soothed by our interactions online. The internet allows us to feel as though we are closing in, getting closer and closer to some sort of security and certainty, and it gives us the illusion that our psychological splitting represents reality accurately. But it is all a mirage.

We are capable of more. We can hold complexity. We can live well even knowing that there is no ultimate security that exists in our world, that there is no overcoming our unknowing, that there is no way to find only the right answers.

I remember when I was in middle school, I would struggle and struggle through whatever obscure math concept I was learning (which I would almost certainly never use again), and I would spend hours doing all of this work and then flip to the back of the book to check my work because that's where literally all of the right answers were. As much as any of us want to believe that life is an open book test and that there are answers in the back of the book, it's just not true. Life is complicated, we are all dealing with different experiences and often trying to solve different problems, and just like in math class, we all need to show our work—we can't just pick an answer from the back of the book because it's "right" or popular.

We have gotten into the dangerous habit of pressuring people to align with whatever "back of the book" answers their specific group holds. "Oh, you're an evangelical? These are your answers. And you over there, you're a liberal progressive? Here are your answers." I have witnessed and also participated in this trend, sharing "answers" that I don't understand or know anything about because I feared that not doing so would put me outside of the group I had found a home with. Back to our desire for external authorities: *Maybe I don't need to find my own equations or do my own work—I can just repost Glennon Doyle because she has the answers!* But allowing a tweet from a stranger to serve as the "right answer" is not our best bet at true evolution, true growth, true human community. Our best answers are in the hard and nuanced work we do, and these answers are not one size fits all.

There is a story from my faith tradition that I find myself coming back to often, one of the many anchors I found that allowed me to stay connected to this faith. It is a story from the Bible that has made its way into popular culture and has even become a shorthand reference for what it means to be a good person. It's the story of the Good Samaritan. There's a man walking down the road who is robbed and beaten, left in the road, bloody, naked, broke. Another man comes down the road, sees the bloody, naked person, and crosses to the other side to continue on his way. A second man walks down the road, sees the bloody man, and does the same thing. But then a third man, a Samaritan (from a nation despised by many people in ancient Judea), sees the man and helps him. He cleans the wounds, gets him some clothes, takes him into town, gets him a place to stay, and makes sure that he has what he needs. OK, you get it. So what's the moral of this story? Pretty obvious, right? Be like the third person. Be the Good Samaritan. At least, that is how the story was always told to me: When given the opportunity, be the good person who helps. But the more I live in the real, complicated human world, the more I wonder whether Jesus told this story to remind us that at any given time, we will represent every person in the story. The thieves, the beaten down, the avoiders, and the helpers.

There have been times in all our lives when we've

behaved more like a hero and other times when we've played the villain. We have all been hurt, and we have all hurt. We have all loved, and we have all broken a heart or two. We have fought for healing and reconciliation, and we've all sought revenge. We slide up and down the moral spectrum. But the spiritual and emotional space where we are freed from false binaries and false choices is the space where we can learn how to be human.

I have a friend who loves his grandmother. Their relationship was once like a cliché from a Hallmark Channel movie. She made him spaghetti most days after school, spoiled him on Christmas, snuck him cookies when his parents weren't looking, and was a soft place to land when life felt overwhelming. Now my friend is in his forties, and he and his grandma find themselves in a situation of competing truths: Now that he has grown into the beautiful gay man that he is, they are at an impasse. Her own antiquated ideas about the world and how it is supposed to work are keeping her from loving and embracing her grandson. He is sorting out whether or not this rejection and her homophobia cancel out who she has been his whole life.

Is it a zero-sum game? Can she be a nice grandma and homophobic? Does the niceness cancel out the homophobia? Does the homophobia cancel out the niceness? Is there one right answer in the back of the book? What do we do when the people in our life are nice and racist? Sweet and sexist?

There is no right answer; there is no clean line. Only both/and.

Almost every aspect of my life and identity currently requires me to shed binary thinking and hold more than one truth at the same time.

I was seven years old the first time I heard the N-word. I was playing with a basketball outside, my dad was pulling weeds in the lawn, and a car full of white teenage boys drove by and yelled it at him. I wasn't completely certain about that word or what it meant, but based on my dad's reaction, I knew it was not good. It was hurtful and infuriating, and from that moment on, for the thirty years since that moment, I have been faced with a series of hurtful and infuriating incidents. I remember being in high school and listening as kids read a book out loud with that same word again. I remember being in college when Barack Obama was running for president and white students at my evangelical college protested and shouted because our country was about to elect the Antichrist. I have been told to straighten my hair for job interviews. I have mourned countless days over the reality that so many of the greatest leaders of our time, the greatest leaders this country has ever seen—like Martin Luther King, Jr., Fannie Lou Hamer, and Medgar Evers—never got to realize their full potential. I stood speechless after realizing that Sandra Bland and I were the same age and had the same master's degree, and that truly there was nothing stopping what happened to her from happening to me. I mourned with the world as we let the reality of George Floyd's murder hit us all in our homes. I protested, I marched, I wrote letters to elected officials.

I was eight years old when I was told that only boys

could be on our neighborhood roller hockey team. I was ten years old when I was told that only boys played with, well, all of the toys that I was interested in. I was thirteen the first time someone suggested I shouldn't cut my hair too short, otherwise I wouldn't be able to find a husband. I was fourteen years old in my middle school cooking class when our teacher told us about the importance of being able to keep men happy. I was thirty years old before I had my first woman boss. I have watched as the responsibility for kindness, empathy, and care has been disproportionately placed on women while their leadership abilities have been denied. I have heard the rhetoric that "girls just mature faster than boys" used to excuse anything from everyday bad behavior in school to sexual assault. I have watched women come forward to share their stories of abuse only to be blamed for what they were wearing. I have watched election after election shine a light on how much this country hates women. I watched as the #MeToo movement lit a spark that set entire industries on fire, and yet we still doubt the power of women. We still pay women less, still obsess over what they wear, and question their priorities if they both work and have kids. We question women at every turn, and it is exhausting.

I didn't come out of the closet until I was twenty-seven. I didn't come out publicly until I was thirty. But I remember living in Colorado in 1998 when Matthew Shepard was murdered; I remember the backlash Ellen DeGeneres got when she came out; I remember my parents not wanting me to watch *Will & Grace*. I remember being in church and learning that being gay was a sin, a sin that God hated more than others, apparently. I don't remember the country going up in a rage as queer activists and leaders were murdered, but I do remember quietly reading about them in my room and wondering if I would ever be brave enough to be honest. I remember being in the closet, working at a megachurch when same-sex marriage became legal in all fifty states, and immediately getting an email from my boss reminding us that we believed in the Bible and telling us not to show support for this moment. I remember the first time I held my wife's hand in public and the first time we kissed at a concert when I knew people could see; I wondered why I was scared, and then I remembered sitting in my living room watching the news about Pulse nightclub. I remembered that "God hates gay people" signs were as common as McDonald's billboards. I am thirty-seven years old and I'm still just scratching the surface of queer history, finding queer pioneers, and holding it all as I watch the news of another shooting, this time in a Colorado Springs gay club.

I am a queer Black woman in America, and I say all of this because it is a hard thing to be, and I hate this country for that. I hate this country for how it has treated people of color, for how it has colonized and killed and stripped, and for how it has regarded women as lesser than men, how women have had to fight, fight not to be hanged as witches, fight for the right to vote, fight not to be assaulted then fight to be believed, fight to get paid, and fight to lead. I hate that we have swept so much queer history under the rug, that we are still fighting for rights and to be valued. I hate that drag queens are under attack and that who goes to the bathroom and where has been more of an issue than it should ever have been. I hate the general homophobia here, I hate what it did to my own sense of self, and I hate how many lives we continue to lose because of it.

And I'm also proud of the progress we have made as a country. I am proud to come from so many great leaders and thinkers. I love this country; I love its beauty and ideals; I love cheering for the U.S. women's national soccer team in the World Cup like my life depends on it. I enjoy the freedoms that I engage in, and I believe in the promise of progress. I believe in the power to change—and I have seen change.

I hate this country; I love this country. The two do not cancel each other out: They exist together, they dance with each other, and on different days one will dominate the other. My job is not to reconcile these two realities, or to force a contrived equality between them. All that I can do is allow them both to exist. The grief is there, the hope is there, and so are the anger and sadness, and the joy and pride. It is all there, all at once, and all I can do is hold all of it. And I want to keep all of it. I *get* to keep all of it. There is not one right way for me to think about America, nor is there one answer for how I should respond to what happens in America. The joy does not cancel out the pain; the grief does not cancel out the hope.

Holding contradictory truths does not diminish my dedication to fighting for what is right. I am still very committed to the work of antiracism, and to fighting for the kind of feminism that will empower women—all women. I will still do everything I can to advocate for queer rights. Shedding binary thinking and holding more than one truth at a time does not change the work that lies ahead, nor does it change my commitment to the work. But as I sit with complexity and take in the nuances of real life, my approach to the work will change—and change for the better.

As my siblings and I were growing up, my dad used to always tell us, "You can't give what you don't have." More often than not, it was true, and it continues to ring true to me today. When it comes to the empathy we must show and the nuance we must permit in order to live in community, we must first learn to be compassionate toward ourselves and allow nuance in our own lives. If we can remember what it feels like to grieve and to have joy, and if we can think back to the choices we have made, how hard they were, and how we fought for the life we have, then we can imagine that every person is probably having a similar experience.

My work changes when I am able to remember that I once sat where my opponents now sit. I once sat in a room of young girls, talking to them about purity. I once believed that being queer was a sin. This history doesn't stop me from wanting to make change, to shift the narrative, and to stop the harm, but it does make it harder to see people as prehistoric, patriarchal idiots incapable of human connection and change. After all, they are just me fifteen years ago. When we can begin to hold and embrace the nuance that exists within us and our lives, then we begin to hold it for others, and truly, that is when we will see change happen.

I am not writing this book for extremists. I am talking to the massive middle, to the folks who are dissatisfied with the current social process and who think we can do better as people. I think there are a lot of us who want to see healing, who want to feel allowed to hold nuance. We are not the loudest, or even the most popular, but I do think we are massively underestimated.

2

Internet Brain

A FEW YEARS AGO, I WAS WATCHING A DOCUMENTARY ABOUT "flat-earthers," people who believe the Earth is flat. The man hosting the documentary went to a flat-earther conference, and there, in the conference room of a Hilton hotel, a few hundred people attended multiple presentations with speakers arguing that scientists have been wrong and that the Earth is, in fact, flat. I was in awe of their commitment. How, in the face of vast evidence to the contrary, were all of these people so committed to the idea that the Earth is flat? The filmmaker interviewed several people in order to answer that same question, often arguing with them, but then one interview left him unsure how to respond. It started off like all of the others, with the documentarian offering a laundry list of scientific evidence that the Earth is round, and the interviewee giving some of the same canned answers the rest of the group had. But then this man shrugged his shoulders and said, "You know what? It's really hard to make friends. And here, I get to go to two conferences a year, chat with a bunch of friends online, and really feel like I belong to something." It was one of the most honest things I have ever heard. This man may not have really believed the Earth is flat, but I don't think he cared either way; he was longing for community, and he had found a group of people with whom he felt he belonged.

This man's experience is a startling reminder of our need and desire for community and human connection. He was willing to ignore evidence and to adopt a set of beliefs if it meant he could be connected to other human beings. I guarantee you that he is not the first and that he won't be the last person to sacrifice truth in order to belong.

In college, I was on the step team. We weren't just a group of girls that performed every once in a while; we were a sisterhood, and I had thirteen built-in best friends throughout my entire college experience. Being a part of the step team was one of my biggest sources of pride and joy because wherever I went, I was a part of that group. If I walked into a party and saw one of my sisters there, then I knew I wouldn't be alone. Walking through campus and hearing someone give our call was a reminder that I belonged to something. On days we would perform and show up in our cute matching outfits, I felt untouchable. These were my sisters. That sense of belonging and community gave me a sense of calm, confidence, and security that I would not have had without that group. That group became a part of my identity; the girls from this team were the same ones standing with me at my wedding, and they have been standing with me ever since.

Lucky for me, there was nothing I had to believe in to be a part of the group, no ideology about life or the world I had to subscribe to. I just had to make sure I showed up to practice on time and didn't mess up the steps. It was a fairly low barrier to entry. My experience with that group, with the people who became my dearest friends, helps me understand why the man in the flat-earther documentary could set aside reason and agree that the Earth is flat—it allows him to be a part of something. And being a part of something gives him confidence and calm and security. But his experience and choice should give us pause. What are the true costs of belonging and feeling secure and confident when belonging entails letting go of vital truths?

In 1989, the psychologist Arie Kruglanski coined the term "cognitive closure." It refers to the point at which our brains decide that enough information has been gathered to make a decision. The concept of cognitive closure is necessary for our survival because our life is a never-ending series of decisions. We wake up and we have to decide what to wear, whether or not to stop at Starbucks on the way to work, what to eat for lunch. On a larger scale, we decide what to do on the weekends, who to date, if we want to get married, and so on. We decide and decide and decide, and for a good portion of our life and in many ways, cognitive closure is helpful. We need cognitive closure, but it can also be extremely dangerous. Our need for closure means that all of us have the potential to become extreme. We crave certainty because we couldn't function without it, but the problem, according to Arie Kruglanski, is that the way we process information and make decisions is different in different circumstances, and during times of uncertainty, everyone's need for closure increases. Sometimes, our need for closure tricks us into thinking we have the truth even when we haven't examined sufficient evidence.

It's important for us to understand how cognitive closure works under pressure because we are living with a lot of uncertainty. Many of us used to think we knew how the world worked or understood the story of our history and what it meant to be an American, and we felt relatively certain about the future of our economy, and of our health and safety. Few of us feel that certainty anymore. And now our uncertainty breeds fear, and the fastest way to manage fear is to latch on to anything that promises simplicity and certainty.

As you read those words, you might have in mind a person, politician, social issue, or news channel that you feel is exploiting the human need for closure. We might associate this tendency with extremism, but we'd be letting ourselves off the hook too easily if we think it's just the extremists who aren't able to have a real dialogue or take in new information. So while I saw cognitive closure in the flat-earther documentary, I have also seen it countless times on social media and around my own dinner table.

Polarization is related to psychological "splitting," which I discussed earlier. Our need to belong to a community, combined with our drive to find cognitive closure, makes us highly susceptible to the extreme ideological polarization that we see every day as politicians and public figures promise a simplicity and security that is not fully realizable. But the cost of believing these promises is that you become unable to take in new information.

At this point, you might be wondering how to differentiate polarization from fighting for a just cause. Because like I said, I am a Black queer woman in America. I have a fight in me, and I believe that I am fighting against injustice, which means I have to fight it with conviction. I believe to the core that Black people are valuable, loved, and deserving of justice and respect like every other person on this earth, and I am not open to hearing any arguments otherwise: I am cognitively closed, and I don't believe this position represents extremism. But what's the difference? How can we know which is which?

Even in extreme polarization, there has to be some common ground in shared reality. There has to be a baseline of belief in human dignity, and when there is, we can escape premature cognitive closure by cultivating the ability to differentiate our core beliefs (for example, human dignity for all) from the secondary applications of those beliefs. For example, we might argue that our present-day response to a long-standing history of white supremacy should be based on preferential discrimination that assists and aids historically oppressed people in attaining the same amount of political and economic power as their white counterparts who have benefited from these inherited advantages. In this example, the core belief of human dignity is not up for debate, while the latter, secondary argument could be rejected while still holding and affirming the former. It is only the extremists who believe that secondary applications cannot be debated.

This is the impasse where a lot of the dialogue we hear today finds itself. Escaping polarization has to involve a willingness to take in new information about secondary or tertiary matters. So we may feel cognitively closed about *what* a truth is (for example, all humans have dignity), but the process of *how* it plays out or should take shape in our world will constantly move and shift.

On the other hand, when communities disagree about core principles like "all people are created equal," then polarization becomes a painful but also necessary step in the process to realize that shared community has been lost. This is what we saw happen with the American Civil War, and in some ways we are witnessing this happen again. When something fundamental is at stake, when a common shared reality of human dignity is on the table, then the community will fracture.

We can and should hold true to our primary and core beliefs about humans and dignity, and yes, when those are denied, we must reject that part of the community that denies them. But our ability to differentiate our core beliefs from our secondary ideas—our understanding of separating the *what* from the *how*—will keep us out of the claws of extremism that seem so ready to grab us all. Be cognitively closed on the core, then be open to natural moves and shifts—new ideas and new experiences can and should change our secondary beliefs.

When asked what stands on the other side of cognitive closure, Arie Kruglanski says that the only alternative is "the abyss." Unfortunately, "Come into the abyss with me" sounds a lot less appealing than "Hey, we have all the right answers."

What we believe can and usually does change. If I went back and read you one of my journal entries from ten years ago, we would both laugh, cringe, and probably cry. I remember one year my wife and I were cleaning out our garage, and she found a journal from high school that she had filled with letters to her future husband—talk about changing ideas.

I do not have all of the answers to know the difference between fighting for a just cause and being swept up in extremism, but I have learned to make room for healthy suspicion about my own righteousness. We have all changed; it would be reckless and naïve to think that at any point we are done changing, done growing. I think it is great to have a guiding set of principles and to fight for the things we believe in, but I also know that I've made lots of mistakes and assumed things I shouldn't have in my own quest for righteousness, certainty, and belonging.

When cognitive closure meets psychological splitting into the poles of good and bad—in religious terms, righteousness—and then we take these tendencies into social media, the result is what I call "internet brain." Internet brain is what allows us to feel as if we have all of the right information and, based on a snapshot of someone else's life, that we know all we need to know in order to make a determination about that person. It's the feeling that all there really is to a person is what we have already seen and that what we have seen confirms what our own group says about the person and their group. Internet brain also leads us to trust our own groups enough to agree with them on issues without having to think about something carefully ourselves—beliefs become a matter of group allegiance, and we will believe what we have to in order to avoid the sting of not belonging.

I have experienced this tension within myself. There have been groups online and in real life that I desperately wanted to be a part of, and that desire to belong made me question myself. *Am I radical enough? Is what I feel good enough? Can I say that? Can I believe this? What is everyone else saying?*

On June 25, 2021, the news broke that Derek Chauvin had been found guilty of the murder of George Floyd. It was a murder that had poured gasoline on the flames of antiracist movements all over America and the world. George Floyd's life, and his absolutely unwarranted death, sparked conversations, books, protests, and vigils. It was a turning point for many people. That a life (and not only his) had to be taken to get our attention anchored the whole racial justice movement in tragedy. What was clear to us was that George Floyd's murderer was guilty. We knew it because we saw it. We watched on our phones; we held that story in our hands. Still, this country does not have a strong track record when it comes to justice for Black lives, and so a lot of people, myself included, doubted that we would see Chauvin held accountable. And when, after a summer of revolution, the verdict was announced, I was shocked by my own reaction. But before I share that, let me remind you of the social mood at the time.

There was pressure from all sides online for people to take some sort of stand. Many people posted a black square on Instagram, some companies posted statements committing themselves to antiracism, and people said things like "Silence is complicity." It felt as though people had their feet firmly planted, and if someone took one step out of line, they were next on the chopping block. It felt as if our whole society was yearning for cognitive closure and the relief certainty brings. A friend I had known for a few years, and whom I had never known to use this kind of language or to talk about these topics, shared an Instagram post, "Ten Steps to Non-optical Allyship." When I texted her to ask what she thought of what she'd shared, she confessed, "I haven't read it yet, and I don't know what non-optical allyship is, but literally everyone is posting that article right now." She had fallen into the frenzy. But that was the environment we were participating in.

It was a wild time online. A lot of good was happening. Everyone was talking, and in some ways, it felt hopeful. But I also wondered if the internet was a place where people could genuinely have these kinds of conversations. Inevitably, online commenters drifted from sharing information and engaging in dialogue to posting critique and criticism from all sides. The articles went from "Ten Things to Know About _____" to "Ten Things Wrong with _____." The cognitive closure was on full display, and it felt as though everyone was reaching for the nearest voice that might offer them some safety, security, and certainty.

When I learned that George Floyd's murderer had been found guilty, and before I could formulate my own thoughts or feelings, I ran to my phone, frantically opened Instagram, and started posting on my story:

"Guilty" with praise hand emojis?

No, just "guilty."

No, say something more meaningful, something deeper . . .

Talk about what you are feeling.

Wait, what am I feeling?

I think I know what I'm feeling, but let me see what other people are saying first to see if what I'm feeling is right.

On one profile: "We shouldn't be celebrating. George Floyd should still be alive."

OK, I shouldn't be happy.

On another profile: "Don't let anyone tell you not to celebrate in this moment. This is the justice we have been waiting for."

Oh, OK, so I can be happy?

Yet another: "This is not justice, this is accountability. They are not the same."

OK, that sounds good—maybe I'll just repost that because I have to say something right now.

I did this for a while, and I reposted and deleted a few

things, until finally I closed the app, looked at my wife, and said, "I actually just feel like I want to cry." So I sat on the couch and cried with my wife. No words, no explanations, no one to critique my tears.

In a moment that signified to me more than just one victory for justice, but a whole history of pain and of yearning for that pain to be recognized, I went to everyone else before I went to myself. I had internet brain.

In my nearly twenty years of being on social media, I have gone through everything from trying to project a perfect life to trying to cultivate conversations, looking to other people for validation, trying to be a "thought leader," and lately, making sure I don't mess up enough to be put on the chopping block.

In my twenties, when I was a pastor at a megachurch, I progressively experienced a feeling that was hard to compare to anything else I'd ever felt. This experience has made me empathetic toward any megachurch pastor out there who is at the center of a hurricane of scandal. It was a feeling of separation. When you are a pastor, there are only a few energies, moods, ways of being that are acceptable for you to show. No matter what was happening, I had to exhibit hope and faith and dependability. No one wanted to go to church and have someone stand on the stage and say, "I'm depressed, God is nowhere to be found, and I need help." The members of the congregation could, and certainly did, feel that way, but honesty about those feelings was out-of-bounds for pastoral staff. (I believe that churches would be in an infinitely better place if pastors could and would be honest.) That inability to be a real human being, that experience of being reduced from a person to a role, and from a member of the community to a living instrument of community maintenance, puts an impenetrable wall around the pastor. You are among people, but you are unreachable and untouchable. Totally separated. And that experience of separation, of having to force myself to project a version of myself that was sometimes at odds with my inner life, broke something in me, and it took a long time to repair that part of myself.

I share this experience I had in ministry because I now recognize that separation when I see it in other people. And the sad thing is that I see that separation all the time now, and it's because of who we allow ourselves to be on the internet and how far removed that is from who we really are. People judge us based on a snapshot that they see online, and we judge others based on a snapshot of them. And even though we know that there is more to us than that, and more to others, the criticisms don't hurt any less, and the consequences aren't any less real.

Social media is a flat (and flattening) space that gives you basic information about where things are, but it cannot tell you anything about what they feel like, how they move and curve. The internet is two-dimensional, while real life is three-dimensional. But we have begun to interact with people as though they are two-dimensional. We tweet things like "If they don't understand you, they don't deserve you," and we repost things like "If your mom isn't in therapy, cut her off." Comment sections are full of statements like "I am a random woman in Kentucky, and I'm here to hold you accountable."

The internet has taken our love for binary thinking and our need for community and mixed the two into a magical potion that seems to have found its way into all our drinking water. Our need for community is what leads us to blindly agree with something, and our love for binaries allows our brains to detach from complex reality.

Stopping internet brain will require a lot from us. It will require us to be open to new information, to tolerate complexity, and to reconcile the fractured parts of ourselves that we have allowed to become disintegrated because of life online. Our real lives and relationships are waiting to be explored, with all of their three-dimensional depths and curves.

3

Forgetting Progressive Amnesia

I F YOU HAD ASKED ME IN 2004 WHO MY HEROES WERE, WHO I was inspired by, and who I wanted to be like, I would have said, without hesitation, Dave Chappelle and Kanye West. Kanye's first album, *The College Dropout,* had just come out and I knew every single word. *Chappelle's Show* was in its second season and, in my opinion at the time, it was some of the most brilliant comedy I had ever seen. The art that those two men created in my formative years shaped a lot of the dreams and goals I would have in the following years. I have always been creative, and for a long time growing up, I couldn't figure out what kind of creative I wanted to be. I didn't want to be like anyone else I saw until I saw these two.

Later that year, I went to a concert at a small theater

in Denver, Colorado, to see Kanye West perform. He wore a pink polo shirt and a Louis Vuitton backpack for the entirety of the show, and it just felt different from anything else I had ever experienced. It inspired me, and it pushed me to think outside the box of what I knew. Up until that point in my life, I had never seen a rapper wear polo shirts and backpacks, and I didn't hear anyone else addressing the things that he was making music about: He challenged and expanded my assumptions about what is possible to create. And then there was Dave Chappelle. My older brother bought me the first season on DVD. (Remember DVDs?) My mind was blown. My nineteen-year-old self could barely handle the irreverence, the jokes, the storytelling; there were so many things about that show that were familiar but also totally new and fresh. I would lie in bed and wonder how on earth he came up with the idea to do a sketch about a Black man who was blind, didn't know he was Black, and became a member of the KKK. Whose brain worked like that? I was enamored with these two creators and the way they seemed to blow past all boundaries of what was expected of them and their crafts. They pushed the envelope, and they created incredible experiences for their fans. I started to study them, to watch their every interview, to read magazine articles about them, to be the first one to buy the new album or watch a new season. I was a fangirl.

A lot has changed since 2004. Those two men no longer stand at the top of my heroes list, and to be honest, I've been appalled by Ye's antisemitic, anti-Black rhetoric and Chappelle's anti-trans comedy. It is not just that I grew out of my fangirl stage; it was that I felt mortified that I was ever in it. It's not like when you discover a new restaurant and you become obsessed, can't get enough, and then eventually feel tired of it. This was more like finding a restaurant, becoming obsessed with it, and then learning that you were actually eating Play-Doh. I wasn't connecting with anything they were saying—I became repulsed by the things they were putting into the world. We all grew and evolved, but we had different trajectories.

Have you ever rewatched an old favorite movie that you've not seen in a long time? Have you ever thought or heard someone else say, "That movie doesn't really hold up"? It means that this piece of art, this narrative, which once fit comfortably in your world, no longer fits. Not too long ago, I rewatched Disney's animated *Peter Pan* movie from 1953. I still know all the words to the songs. Well, in case you haven't seen *Peter Pan* in a while, let me just tell you right now: It doesn't hold up. The treatment of indigenous people and their culture in this movie is startling. And it wasn't that long ago that the movie was a household treasure.

Speaking of things that don't hold up: One night in 2010, I sat in a small theater on a college campus. The theater was packed to near capacity, with first- and second-year college students, all of them young women. They piled into the theater because a group of us "older" women (and by "older" I mean they were nineteen and we were twenty-four) told them we had important things to say about what it means to be a woman, about sisterhood. And they believed us. We put on a full night of programming; we had music, lights, and speakers, and lucky for me, I got to close the show. After the music got everyone in their feels, after the lights had gotten progressively dimmer, it was my time to shine. I was the hopeful external authority of the night, and I had an opportunity to say something important— something meaningful, something that would feel like balm for the soul.

So what did I say to the two-hundred-plus students packed in this theater? Did I tell them to burn down the patriarchy? Did I tell them about their inherent value and worth? Did I tell them that being a woman is one of the greatest gifts you can receive from the Creator and that they should cherish it and not let anyone diminish it? Did I use that time to remind them that all women are women, to never forget to include trans women in our beloved community? No, I didn't say any of that. I got up there and I gave a message about purity. I talked about waiting until marriage to have sex: literally something I couldn't care less about today, and something I certainly had no business caring about then. But that's the message I gave—and it went great. There were lots of tears and applause, and these young girls came up to me after to thank me. Why? Because we had all drunk the same Kool-Aid, and we were conditioned to believe that a random twenty-something-year-old woman standing on a stage telling slightly younger women not to have sex until they got married was completely normal. It makes my skin crawl every time I think about it. How many of those women have sat in a therapist's office in the last ten years and said, "This one night, in this theater, this speaker told me something and it still haunts me to this day"? Purity culture has ruined lives and sex lives, and has contributed to wild abuse of power by men, and I was a participant in that. My own life is a movie that doesn't hold up.

But I have grown up, I have learned and found a bigger story of humanity, and these things no longer fit. And not only do they not fit, but I will do my best to continue expanding my understanding of life and to help dismantle the corrupt systems and ideas that have given these false narratives so much power. I will not play any part in these ideas—anymore. I no longer believe what I once did, but I also cannot pretend that it never happened. I am very connected to the version of me that used to believe these things. I understand her, I grieve with her, she has my empathy, and I think some of the most important work I can do is to stay close to her and remember how it felt to be her. That connection is what I want to be guiding me as I move forward in this work.

I think a lot of us suffer from something I call progressive amnesia. We magically and conveniently forget about the time before we came to know what we know now. We forget what it was like to be super Christian, before we understood how to use correct pronouns, before we knew there was racism in our understanding of the world. Our brains seem to go blissfully blank when we are asked to recall a time before now. We learn something new and then immediately begin acting as if we have known it forever.

When I was in middle school, a very hot new band arrived on the scene (and the scene was suburban Colorado, so I am sure they hit better scenes long before then), a band called Blink-182. One day a friend at school asked me if I knew who they were, and I admitted I did not. I still remember the scolding laughter in his voice: "You don't know who Blink-182 is?" After that, I asked around, got some information from my neighborhood friends, and at a grocery store found a *People* magazine with an article about Blink-182. I was with my mom, who wasn't going to buy the magazine for me, so I quickly consumed as much information as I could before the groceries were bagged. Armed with literally the least amount of information possible, I was a little more prepared for the next time I might be questioned about this band. And the very next day I overheard someone talking about how much they loved Blink-182, and another girl asked, "Who is Blink-182?" There it was, my time to shine. Before I could even blink (pun intended), I shamed her with the same scolding laugh I was subjected to just the day before: "Oh my God, you don't know who Blink-182 is?" I could see the embarrassment in her face, the same I had felt, but now here I was, standing on my high horse—a horse of three skimmed pages of a *People* magazine. Welcome to progressive amnesia.

Progressive amnesia is the tendency to forget (conveniently!) our own lapses and learning trajectories. It's what happens when we disconnect from our personal growth histories and allow ourselves to forget our own pasts.

It infects people who overlook the many times they have

made mistakes and how long it took to overcome their ignorance and do better. It is what tempts a person to join a self-righteous internet mob and judge other people as if it is their job.

Let's see if this scene sounds familiar.

Let's say we have a friend named Lisa, and Lisa is wanting to cut back on dairy because her stomach has been acting funny. Lisa goes to a coffee shop and orders a latte with almond milk for the first time. She's so excited about her new almond milk journey that she takes a cute picture of her latte and posts it online. Chaos ensues.

The first person to comment is another woman who, two hours prior, read an article about unfair coffee farming practices. She writes, "All the almond milk in the world can't cover the blood on your hands from drinking at Starbucks, Lisa."

Lisa, unaware of the article her internet friend stumbled upon earlier that morning, replies curiously, "Wait, what's wrong with Starbucks?"

A new person joins the comments, who only five minutes ago heard that almond trees are causing a water shortage in California. They comment, "The problem is that while you're busy thinking about coffee farmers, your almond milk is killing the earth and soon there will be no planet to farm—did you ever think about that?!"

The first person replies, "Wow, so you're saying almonds are more important than human lives?"

A third person has an even hotter take: "Wow, both of you are completely missing the mark because it's not about the farmers or the almonds, it's capitalism, and if you can't see that then I guess you're just another pawn in the capitalist scheme—and that actually makes me sad because I thought you were both smarter than that."

Finally, a fourth person reading along, this one a peripheral acquaintance of Lisa's, feels compelled to join in: "Hey, Lisa, so sorry to see that you're not a conscious consumer of coffee or almonds. I'd hoped we could build a friendship, but after reading these comments and seeing your lack of response here, it makes me wonder if you're even the type of person I want to follow on here. I'm gonna go, and I hope you find the resources to educate yourself about what's really important."

Lisa is now in tears, not drinking her latte.

We all know Lisa. We have either been her or been the people in her comments. We have all seen people comment as though they were born with all of the information they now have.

Progressive amnesia was on full display in the summer of 2020. In my opinion, this phenomenon disproportionately affected white women. That summer was when a lot of people were confronted with the reality of racism in America, and for a lot of folks, it was for the first time. Even though racism is pervasive, it's designed not to be seen. If you benefit from white privilege, one of the privileges is that you don't have to see that privilege. But here we were, as a country, face-to-face with one of our deepest and most pervasive evils, and people were starting to wake up. There were conversations around dinner tables, documentaries and news stories, and antiracism books flying off the shelves. It was a terrifyingly beautiful time. Everyone seemed to want to know more so that we could collectively do better. But something else was also happening. The progressive amnesia was setting in and setting in fast. I started seeing lots of white women on the internet going full *WWE Smackdown* in comments sections, calling out the racism of other white women when a very quick glance at their own profiles revealed that they had only joined this conversation two weeks earlier.

And listen, I'm not saying you can't call out racism, but when you have the equivalent amount of information that I had after a forty-five-second speed-read of a *People* magazine, maybe you can get off your high horse and invite people into the same conversation you just joined yesterday. Did these women on the internet not remember the three weeks prior when they didn't even know racism was an issue? But now they were in the comment sections living out their full social justice warrior fantasy. Again, I am not saying that our connection to ourselves and to our mistakes takes us out of the work, but I hope that it can change our approach to the work. What would it have looked like if, instead of sending that girl who asked about Blink-182 into the same shame storm I had been through, I had said, "Oh girl, don't trip. I just found out who they were yesterday— it's a band." Would that have been so hard? Would that have been any less "effective"? Why didn't I just do that? Why didn't more people on social media say things like "Hey, I actually just found out yesterday that the language I used for a long time is no longer appropriate. Let me know if you want the reading list that helped me get there"?

One driver of progressive amnesia is our desire to bypass our own feelings. It allows us to outsource our emotional labor to strangers on the internet. It provides us instant, although not lasting, relief from the discomfort that comes with admitting to having supported something that you now realize was harmful or corrupt. Rather than sitting with the truth of your own history, it's easier to project judgment onto the faceless people of the internet. James Baldwin puts it this way: "I imagine that one of the reasons people cling to their hates so stubbornly is because they sense, once hate is gone, that they will be forced to deal with pain."

It is painful to outgrow ideas and beliefs you once held, agonizing to know that you have contributed to harm, and gut-wrenching to realize that some of the evils of this world have persisted because of your complicity. That pain is real, and for that pain there is no easy comfort. We know from cognitive closure that the more change and uncertainty we face, the more we crave certainty, and that believing you're right feels like certainty. But we cannot bypass the pain and the self-examination and jump straight into being right; our ability to sit with this discomfort will also make all the difference in how we approach the work. For white women in this country, I imagine the anger, the rage, and the shame of watching (and rewatching) the unjust murders of Black Americans, listening to news stories, and hearing the chants of protest. The horror they felt as their eyes opened for the first time. When I feel that kind of pain, my first instinct is to get rid of it, to pawn it off. That summer of 2020, the conversations I heard and read online felt like lots of people screaming, "*I am hurting, and I want you to hurt, too!*" At my best, I want people to find healing because I have found it. But at my most reckless, I want people to hurt because I hurt.

Richard Rohr wrote something that has absolutely been glued to me since the day I read it. Have you ever read something so true it makes you a little angry? That's how I felt reading these words he wrote: "If you don't transform your pain, you transmit your pain."

I'm sorry to have to tell you this, but your emotional pain is yours to deal with. My emotional pain is mine to deal with. Our anger, our shame, our pain—we can do our best to pawn it off on our neighbors, or we can do the work to hold it, to feel it, to understand it, to grieve with it, to grow with it, to let it ride in the car with us, and to see how it might change our direction.

I know what it's like to want someone to feel shame because I feel it. I know what it's like to want someone to hurt because I am hurting. I know the difference between wanting revenge and wanting justice. I know what it is to feel like I am bad, and to treat everyone the same way, and I know what it feels like to believe so deeply in my own dignity that I have no option other than to believe in the dignity of every other human being.

The good news is that progressive amnesia doesn't have

to be permanent. This is not a terminal diagnosis. But the harder news is that to reverse this condition requires sitting with your own pain.

I once had a therapist describe my pain to me as a spiral staircase. I will be on it forever, but the hope is that with each new year or season, I am able to see it from another perspective. I can test to see if my ideas about it "still hold up." I can find new vantage points, and I can engage with it in a new way, but one thing is certain: Pain will always be there. Joy and pain are inevitable; how we let them shape our time is up to us. I don't want to forget what it was like to be me ten years ago, and I don't want to pretend that I never believed the things I used to believe. I want to fight the power structures in our world knowing what it feels like to live within those structures and even to work for them. It does not change the work at hand, but I am convinced it changes our approach. You don't need to pretend that you know all the right things and that you always have, and you don't have to pretend that there are no parts of your story that don't hold up. You don't have to avoid the pain of what you have said and done before you know what you know now. Acknowledging that pain, and sitting with that version of yourself, is what will create a world where more people can go on the journey you have gone on. What you do with your pain can create more healing, more transformation, and more evolution, and that is what we all desperately need.

When we reconnect to the versions of ourselves that we have outgrown, and when we remind ourselves that we had much to learn, we are freed to let go of the judgmentalism and self-righteousness that craves a sacrifice. Overcoming progressive amnesia doesn't mean abandoning accountability. It means learning to see the humanity that connects us to others, even those who behave in disappointing ways, and understanding that an invitation is often far more powerful than a cancellation.

4

Whatever You Do, Don't Get Canceled

I HAVE BEEN A BIG FAN OF COMEDY FOR AS LONG AS I CAN remember. In high school, my friends and I would put on fake stand-up comedy shows in the basement of one of our houses. We would pretend to do crowd work to the empty couches in front of us. I would watch all of the great HBO stand-up specials, the one where Eddie Murphy is wearing that wild red leather outfit, Robin Williams, Chris Rock, the aforementioned Dave Chappelle. Comedy felt like a lot of other places in my life where I saw something I wanted to do, or someone I wanted to be, but where I noticed that women were rarely present. Sparse but not invisible. I remember watching Sarah Silverman and the first time I read something Margaret Cho had written. Wanda Sykes made me laugh so hard that Sprite came out my nose one day, and of course Tina Fey and Amy Poehler are two of the funniest people I've ever seen. Comedians have always found a way to make things we all experience hilarious, and that is my favorite thing about comedy. Ellen told a joke in a recent special about how many books we take on vacation; we don't read any books at home, but we somehow think we are going to read nine books on a beach in Mexico. It's funny because it's true, it's relatable, it's insightful.

Comedy adds levity to the parts of our lives that otherwise feel mundane or even heavy. Comedy can give us all a common laugh, and that laughter creates space where there was once tension. Laughter is the absolute best way to connect a room of people, and it is one of my favorite things in the world. Comedy has also been used to push boundaries, and parody and satire have been used to mock our experinces. Comedy can offend—often intentionally. In the past few years, however, I've noticed an interesting energy in a lot of comedy spaces: The content has become stale, and there is more whining than joking. The thing that used to bring levity has become an instrument to air grievances. Where there was once freedom, there is now fear.

The reasons for this shift are partly understandable. Comedians have always pushed boundaries. They have said things that make people think, make people squirm, and hopefully make people laugh. There have long been comedians who blow right past what is appropriate, respectful, or decent, and there have been essentially no consequences for someone who disregards human feelings and experiences in the name of a good joke. There has long been little to no accountability in the comedy world either for actions offstage or words said onstage, and it shows. In the last few years, however, we saw, across multiple platforms, some truly awful behavior come to light, and those people were held accountable. We also started to have language for and to build some barriers around what was appropriate for someone to say, and some of the people (let's be honest, mostly men) who were exposed for their behavior or who faced accountability for the jokes they told at the expense of others did not take it well. This group of comedians who, for long periods of time, had seemingly free rein over their language and behavior, and who relished their ability to be irreverent, now found themselves on the losing end of cancellations and Netflix walkouts, and that reality brought anger. And beyond the anger, the fear was almost palpable.

What were they afraid of? Well, on one hand, some truly horrendous behavior was exposed, and those people will never tell a joke in public again—thankfully. On the other hand, some comedians fell somewhere in the middle of the road; they had not committed sexual assault, but they had definitely told a questionable joke or two in the past few years, and as these comedians watched some of the pillars of comedy fall, the fear leaked all over their art. Watching titans fall was sending a shiver down lots of spines in the comedy world.

I found myself in 2022 at a comedy show in Los Angeles. The venue was packed to the absolute brim. Every other year, Netflix hosts the Netflix Is a Joke Fest, a marathon of comedy shows in L.A. It is one of my favorite events because the entire city is buzzing with comedy shows. Tiny theaters, big stadiums, shows in the park—all over the place, our city is filled with people daring to find some levity and relatability and bring people together. One night, I went to the most packed show I had been to during the festival, where ten comedians were on the roster. I was excited. The first comedian, a white man, got on the stage and said something to the effect of "Comedians are under attack right now." He talked about how he can't joke about anything these days without getting canceled. To me, he sounded like a whiny baby, but to my surprise, more than a few thousand people erupted into loud applause and cheers for his babyish comments. Then the next comedian came up, and he started his set with similar sentiments: "I remember when comedians could actually be comedians." Again, cheers and applause. This happened about five more times before I stopped being surprised and started getting curious. These people who are tasked with the incredible job of finding levity in the mundane, of making us think by making us laugh or giving us a common breath, were all of a sudden just standing onstage complaining—and people were agreeing with them? What was this? Why did everyone feel bad for these guys? Why did their feeling of being attacked feel relatable to this very progressive audience of Los Angeles comedy fans? What have we created?

It was a relatively grim night of comedy, and it was also the night I realized that what we have created in the celebrity world has spilled into the regular world. Were we making better behavior, or were people just now too scared to be honest? These comedians feeling sad they can't make offensive jokes is one thing, but thousands of Angelenos cheering them on in solidarity? What the heck was that about? What were they afraid of?

One of my biggest grievances with the social pressure we have put on people to be right is that people have become afraid of the wrong thing.

The internet and social media have made it exponentially easier to have your insufficiencies, flaws, antiquated ideology, and biases exposed for the whole world to see, and when they are exposed you will find yourself on your knees, head held firmly in the guillotine of public opinion. The consequences of finding yourself there, on your knees, may cost you friends, reputation, and even career. We all know the process when it comes to our famous friends: We love a celebrity, then we hear them say something racist or homophobic, or a picture surfaces of them dressed as an indigenous person for Halloween. Then the public strikes. We get them taken off shows, we stop buying their books, we pressure their employers and their professional colleagues and friends to make a statement about them. We strip them of everything they have, and then we move on to the next.

The fascinating thing about this cycle is that what started with celebrities, what started with hearing people like DaBaby go on absolutely appalling anti-gay rants and getting him kicked off of every major music festival for that year, taught us something—it created connections in our brains. We all started to think this was normal behavior, and we started taking it everywhere with us. Most people now know that you do not need to be a celebrity to be absolutely thrown into the ring of public opinion, and the likelihood of losing friends, opportunity, and community is just as great for you as it is for celebrities. And sure, maybe we have slightly better behavior for it, but I don't believe the change is going to be real or long-lasting, because I think a lot of people are afraid of the wrong thing.

I think a lot of people are more afraid of being perceived as racist than they are of actually being racist. And that is a problem. Our survival now rests on our ability to hide—and not our ability to learn something new. That should terrify all of us. I have no problems with actions having consequences, and I love that more people with microphones are feeling more conscious of how they use them, but the game has become "don't get canceled," not "be a good person," and it shows. We have struck the wrong chord of fear, and it is one that will unfortunately not last. Nothing will kill a movement faster than thousands of people pretending that they support it. What good will it do to have a bunch of entertainers too afraid to get onstage and tell the jokes that they are certainly still telling in their living rooms? What good will it do to terrorize a teenager into silence when they lack a basic understanding of why what they did was wrong? How long will the shame of a public flogging keep someone on their best behavior?

There was a 2022 story in *New York* magazine called "Canceled at 17." The story tracked a high school student named Diego who was experiencing what started as accountability but quickly morphed into annihilation.

Diego made a big mistake; he did something wrong, and that is very important information for the story. He was dating a girl, also in high school, and she had sent him a private photo. Diego, drunk at a party, showed that photo to a few friends. Big mistake, right? Yes. So what happens now? Well, long story short, it was dealt with by the principal and parents, but at some point word got around to the other students. The response was frenzied. A group of students got together, dissatisfied with the accountability in this and previous similar cases, and made a list of names. They painted them on the walls of the girls' bathrooms, and over the list they wrote, "Get abusers off campus." The students also organized a walkout; they said that as long as Diego went to school there, they wouldn't be there. They tormented him at every turn. He lost his job, friends, and community. Eventually, he connected with other students who had been canceled that year at that school. One girl whose boyfriend's name appeared on the list of abusers stayed with him, and so she found herself on the list next. Turns out, her boyfriend's name appeared by accident, but still, the train had already left the station. The fact that Diego attended prom provoked the students into staging another walkout.

Now, this kid made a mistake; he did something extremely inappropriate that should absolutely have consequences and accountability, but I think we would be lying if we didn't acknowledge that the frenzied nature of cancel culture has taken accountability and turned it into annihilation. We now have people living under the fear of punishment and not the desire for change. We no longer trust that our connections with our community are safe. We know that our head can be on a spike as fast as the next person's, and that our connection to other humans may be in jeopardy.

I want change that stems from a desire to be good, not from a fear of punishment. And yes, that change should have accountability and consequences—I believe these things help a person understand the significance of mistakes made. But there is something else fueling our frenzy to want to see people destroyed.

The internet and social media have made it easier to showcase people's flaws. And depending on how outdated, ignorant, or hurtful those flaws may be, a misstep may cost you friendships, hurt your reputation, and limit your career opportunities. No wonder my friends—especially the progressive ones—often feel paralyzed with fear that they might make a wrong move or say the wrong thing and provoke strangers on the internet. The stakes are as high as ever, and there are serious consequences for those who use the wrong terminology, promote the wrong idea, or ask the wrong question. Someone can unearth a decades-old blog post or tweet and ruin your reputation. Ordinary mistakes that were once considered part of growing up might be used to alter another person's life. Now, even writing these words, I feel the tension—*but there is real harm happening.* It's true. There is harm happening, and these things are really bad; offensive jokes contribute to shame and even violence. A girl in high school really did have a private photo of herself shared. I don't want it to seem as though I am saying,

"Things happen, too bad." I am not saying that. Actions demand consequences, and people should be held accountable. However, I am looking at the accountability and asking if this form of it is really going to help us get where we want to go.

This cultural shift has helped bring to the fore urgent social issues and important moral conversations. But it has had the unintended consequence of focusing our attention on others' perceptions about us rather than on our growth areas. From fear, we begin to divert our attention away from what matters most—learning, growing, listening, being better—and to direct our energy to making sure we don't get called out or canceled. I don't want people who are afraid of punishment; I want people who are afraid they may cause harm.

I know there is nuance here and that there is a difference between Louis C.K. and a high schooler. There is a difference between what Dave Chappelle said and what Harvey Weinstein did. There is a difference between someone wearing a Native headdress at Coachella and storming the Capitol on January 6. There is a difference between speech and behavior. All of these are actions that require consequences, but how do we find accountability and not annihilation? For some, there is little difference between the two. Harvey? He's done. But for a Coachella headdress girl? What do we do? Do we release the same kraken on her too? I think it is going to be of the utmost importance that we are able to distinguish harm and offense. I know there are some who would say that all offense is harm or that they are one and the same, but I think that idea is erasing the line between consequences and punishments. The Coachella headdress girl is causing offense but not necessarily harm. An offended person is not necessarily the same thing as a victim. Collapsing the two together is a large part of our issues right now. Responding differently to offense versus harm could allow more room for actual evolution, but we have to be willing to understand and acknowledge the distinction.

I don't want to live in a world where people are more afraid of being perceived as racist than they are afraid of being racist. I don't want to live in a world where people publicly say one thing that they know they should and say other things privately in their living rooms—the things they actually believe. Is there a way to create a world where people feel safe to make mistakes? Yes, I know there is a very big sliding scale of mistakes and that they all have consequences, but I think we can all agree the consequences of the internet do not always fit the crime. So what do we do now?

How can we create a desire to be better that outweighs a fear of getting canceled?

Saying things or working through thoughts and conversations privately with a friend or partner is one of the biggest benefits that relationships have to offer. Sharing beliefs and ideas with my wife that I have not fully formed or am working out, or honestly just telling her any and every random thought that pops into my head, is one of my favorite things about being in community with her, and these kinds of spaces are important for all of us. This kind of open-ness and truth-telling and idea sharing does make it a safer environment to make mistakes in. Being truly known by others allows for a different type of response to be made. I think we have gotten into a situation where we are only seeing people in their mistake-making and without the con-text of who they are or any other things about them. So of course we can respond harshly, because it is of no con-sequence to us. I believe we all need and deserve spaces in our lives where ideas get worked out, where we step in and out of line, where we are known enough to allow someone to hold the edges for us while we wiggle around and find our footing.

The answer to this cannot be "get everything right all of the time," because that is simply impossible. No one was born knowing all that they should know. But I do believe that if we created environments that were safe enough to ask, grow, push to learn, and find our edges, then we would naturally want to keep growing and asking and learning. But if our hands get slapped every time we raise them, then eventually we will stop asking questions, stop growing, and find ourselves cognitively closed and pointing fingers at everyone else. I don't want to get thrown under the bus, but I also want to learn new things, and I know from life experi-ence that learning new things has to come with mistakes.

5

The Lost Art of Making Mistakes

MY STOMACH DROPPED LIKE A SHIP LAYING ANCHOR. ALL of the color left my face and my skin tingled like static on TV from my neck to the top of my head. My hands went clammy like they hadn't since middle school when kids were grinding on each other to the last song at a dance and I was in the corner doing the robot because no one had told me I was gay yet. I couldn't even look over at my wife. I felt so much guilt that it turned into shock. It felt like the biggest mistake I had ever made or would ever make.

My wife started her creative career as a wedding photographer and videographer. I was a pastor at a very inclusive but also very small and poor church, and Sami was just getting started shooting weddings, so yeah, we were broke. I noticed that every time she shot a wedding, she had to pay a good portion of her earnings to hire a second shooter, someone to help capture things she missed and be in all the places she couldn't. After much back-and-forth, I finally convinced her just to take me as her second shooter so we could spend time together and save money—a win-win, right? Granted, I have absolutely no photo or video skills, and I had minimal knowledge of the very expensive camera, but if there is one gift (and curse) that has followed me through this life, it is my use of words, and so somehow I convinced my wife this was a good plan. She gave me a crash course on the camera, and we were off!

This wedding in particular was different from usual; the couple was cool and thought outside the box. They did their wedding in a literal forest underneath trees—it was beautiful. So, my job? I only had one job—literally only one. My wife set up a tripod and the camera in the back of the ceremony and said, "I will be running around getting artsy shots. All you need to do is stand here, push record, and get one view of the entire ceremony." It was at this point that I doubled down on my confidence. *Just stand here and push a button?*

The ceremony starts, and it is one of the most enchanting weddings I have ever seen. There I am standing in the back, doing my one job, with tears rolling down my face (I've never attended a wedding that didn't make me cry—I just love love). At one point, all the guests held hands in a giant circle and sang "Lean on Me" a cappella. There were birds and squirrels, deer stopped by, the sun was shining, it was all so beautiful. I watched my wife running around making sure she caught every ray of sun on the dress, every guest's face as they sang. I was euphoric. The ceremony ended, not a dry eye in the forest, as the bride and groom walked down the aisle and down the trail. My job had ended, so I reached up to stop the recording on my very important camera, and when I pushed the button . . . *it started recording*. I had forgotten to push the button—I never started recording. My one job, my only job.

I looked over at my wife. She was running over to me with a smile on her face that matched the occasion—we had just witnessed what was quite possibly one of the most captivating celebrations of love we would ever see. She was so full of energy, but she took one look at my face and knew something was wrong. My heart somehow found a lower point to sink to as I told her what happened. Tears were filling up my eyelids, and she looked at me very straight-faced and told me to keep it together. Why? Because *we still had to shoot the rest of the day*. We had to go to the reception, the first dance, the cake—we still had to do all of it together while holding the weight of this massive mistake I had made. We had to go on without this couple seeing on our faces that we were holding a secret about their very special day.

I have perhaps never felt worse about anything. My wife eventually forgave me . . . until she had to sit down and email the couple and tell them what happened. She offered them a refund for the video, which put us into an even worse financial position than before. This happened about six years ago, and even writing this story, I feel embarrassed. Mistakes are hard, forgiving yourself for making them is harder, and facing consequences for actions sucks. It's hard, but it's good. It's the business we all need to be in.

We all know the feeling of making mistakes. We have all had moments where our stomach sinks so hard that we think it might fall out. We all know how uncomfortable it is to watch someone else deal with the consequences of our actions.

It takes maturity to own our mistakes. It takes bravery to move on from them.

There is a field by my house with a big concrete loop that goes all the way around it. It makes for a very popular destination for runners, walkers, and friends who just want to catch up as they sip their coffee and walk around the loop. There's also a big empty parking lot where teenagers learn how to drive and where kids learn how to ride their bikes. Sometimes people practice roller-skating. On any given day, this place is buzzing with energy. It's often where I go to clear my head, walk and listen to a podcast, or take my dog to try to tire him out. One day I was feeling particularly overwhelmed with life and there was a podcast I wanted to listen to, so I went to walk the loop and to listen. While I was listening—this episode was about internal family systems and reparenting yourself, and I was neck-deep in thought about all of my coping mechanisms and trauma, feeling very overwhelmed—I looked over to the right. In the field was a grown woman, probably in her forties, with a man about the same age, and they were participating in something that literally sent me into tears. With lots of assistance from her friend, this woman pulled herself up onto the seat of a bike, while the man held the back of the bike seat and ran with her as she wobbled down the field. When she reached a certain speed, her friend let go of the seat, and she took off by herself—his arms were pumping in the air, cheering her on. I watched a grown woman learn to ride a bike that day. I cried all the way back to my car because it felt like the most beautiful and profound thing I had ever seen.

What narratives about herself did she have to give up to reach this moment? What narratives about where she should have been already or what she should have known already did she have to ignore? How many times did she have to fall and get back up before arriving at the wobbly yet significant success that I witnessed? What exists in a person that allows them, against the odds and amid failure, to persist toward the version of themselves they most believe in?

We all know that mistakes are an inevitable part of life and an even more inevitable part of progress. In my work doing antiracism training for organizations, I often see a few different attitudes. One is the very overeager person who has read all the books, is up-to-date on all the most current language, and desperately just wants to get it right. The other posture I often see is that of the person who doesn't want to engage at all for fear of making mistakes. They don't feel confident that they know all the right things, so they stay silent. At the beginning of every session, I say the same thing: "You can either be right or you can be in the work; you can't be both." What I mean is that mistakes are inevitable, that they are necessary, and that you have to get it wrong to learn how to get it right. If you want to be in the business of growth and progress, you have to get familiar with the lost art of making mistakes.

Most of us understand the science behind and the importance of making mistakes when it comes to some of the less emotional aspects of progress and growth. It makes sense to us that falling down on a bike is a fundamentally inevitable part of learning to ride. We cannot imagine that a track athlete learning to run hurdles will never run into them. (Hurdles are so mind-blowing to me. I am never not impressed when I see full-speed running and jumping at the same time.) We know that to become proficient in anything requires us to make mistakes.

We know that mistakes are one of the crucial ways that our brains develop, and I think that (for the most part) we are OK with that. Most of us are willing to make mistakes when it comes to practicing a new skill or painting the walls in our garage or "Oops, I went to the store for oat milk, but I accidentally got almond." We get it, we are OK with it, we learn and adapt and move on. But what makes us so bad at and uncomfortable with other kinds of mistakes?

Well, let's look at some different types of mistakes.

Mindset Works, a company based on the research of Carol Dweck and Lisa Blackwell, has identified four types of mistakes: stretch mistakes, a-ha moment mistakes, sloppy mistakes, and high-stakes mistakes.*

First up we have *stretch mistakes*. These are positive mistakes made by trying to do something beyond what we have been able to previously do successfully. These are the mistakes with high learning opportunities, like learning how to ride a bike or to change our own oil. These are mistakes we make in growth. I think these are some of the most palatable mistakes that we can make. It is obvious to us and our brains that these kinds of mistakes lead to something good, something better.

A-ha moment mistakes. These are positive mistakes that we make in which we realize what we've done is not effective. Early in my career, I had the kind of jobs that required making multiple Excel sheets full of names, email addresses, and phone numbers that needed to be in alphabetical order. I would be given physical sign-up sheets attached to a clipboard, and I was expected to make them not only digital but also alphabetical. I developed a process for this in which I would type all the names in a Word doc, then copy and paste them one by one into alphabetical order. I would have hundreds of names, and I would

† Eduardo Briceño, "Mistakes Are Not All Created Equal," Mindset Works, January 16, 2015, https://community.mindsetworks.com/entry/mistakes-are-not-all-created-equal.

look at a name like "Brian Smith," and say that Smith will be somewhere toward the bottom, then I would copy his name, drag it to the bottom of my Word doc, and do this over and over at an excruciatingly slow pace until I had an alphabetical Word doc. Then (because that wasn't tedious enough already) I would type all the names, emails, and addresses again, only this time I was adding them all one by one into Excel. And then I was done. Easy peasy. One day a co-worker saw me doing this extremely inefficient process that I had already completed for countless lists, and he asked me what I was doing. Once he stopped being both shocked and confused at how much extra work I voluntarily gave myself, he told me that Excel can alphabetize the list for me, and that I had created an extremely time-consuming and unnecessary step in the process. That was an a-ha moment mistake.

Sloppy mistakes. These are mistakes we make by losing focus doing something that we know well. Sloppy mistakes are the ones when we cut our fingers chopping garlic or leave the coffee cup on the top of our car—we just get sloppy doing our everyday tasks. Sloppy mistakes are probably the ones we make on the most consistent basis. Some sloppy mistakes have a higher impact than others. Leaving coffee on the car sucks—sloppy but minimal. Forgetting to hit record and not capturing one of the most important days of someone's life? Sloppy and severe.

By the way, all of these types of mistakes can be minimal or severe. An error while cooking can cause you to use salt instead of sugar, and your cake will taste disgusting, but you will be fine. A sloppy mistake while driving can have far more severe consequences.

The last kind of mistake is the one that takes the most maturity and understanding of ourselves, and the one that requires us to have a well-rounded perspective on the value of mistakes. Taking responsibility for leaving your coffee on top of the car or not knowing how to use Excel is easy. Falling down while learning how to ride a bike is understandable. But high-stakes mistakes? This is where a lot of us can get stuck. Fear of this kind of mistake is what keeps us still, stagnant, and afraid.

High-stakes mistakes are mistakes that we make by taking risks in high-stakes situations—which essentially describes all human relationships. High-stakes mistakes happen when we allow ourselves to be vulnerable in a relationship and it's not reciprocated or held in confidence. High-stakes mistakes are what we make when we think we are doing the right thing, have the right cause, are on the right side of history, but then realize we're not. High-stakes mistakes are the ones that get us canceled on social media; they are the mistakes that have the potential to separate us from our community. Remember, our connection to community and our sense of security are imperative to our experience as humans, so making the type of mistake that risks connection or security is terrifying and far more dangerous than a coffee on the roof of our car. High-stakes mistakes can push us faster toward progress or slow us down to a halt, and our ability to choose between those reactions is some of our most important work.

Have you ever gotten your heart broken? Heartbreak is sort of a universal experience, in my opinion, and it comes in many forms beyond romantic relationships. In my own life, I think one of my biggest and most hurtful heartbreaks came from the church, from my community. I always find it funny that when I am listening to really good heartbreak music—like Adele—and I am singing my heart out, tears welling in my eyes as I drive my car and feel all the pain of heartbreak in her lyrics, I am usually thinking about my relationship with my former church. The relationship that handed me my biggest heartbreak. The most high-stakes mistake I have ever made and one of the biggest growth opportunities I have ever been presented with.

When you are young, you don't always realize how high-stakes the decisions that you make are. I honestly didn't really think twice about attending a small evangelical Christian university because I was committed, and Christians were my community, where I found my sense of belonging. It felt like an honor to be a leader and a pastor in a community that represented my belonging, my home; my most meaningful relationships all centered on my belief in and my belonging to this group. I knew there were parts of me that I had to put to the side to secure my belonging in this group, and that is perhaps high-stakes mistake number one. I also had doubts and questions that I refused to engage with because I didn't want to find out that my belief wasn't as ironclad as I once thought it was. I ignored those questions for a long time, and that is high-stakes mistake number two.

In the aftermath of my being honest, of my being true to who I was and who I loved, in revealing my doubts and questions, my worst fears were realized. The church community did in fact put me to the side, my heart was broken, and I felt loneliness in a way I had never experienced. The loneliness was confusing for a while. Was I sad because of my own mistakes or because of theirs? How could I avoid making such a mistake again? And yet, at the same time, I was holding loneliness and heartbreak in one hand, and love and freedom in the other. It was not all bad; it was the highest high in tandem with the lowest low. I lost and I gained all at the same time, but one thing was for sure—I wanted at all costs to avoid experiencing pain like that again.

My breakup with the church followed the path of a lot of romantic breakups. It started with "I'm honestly not even that sad; if they can't handle me, they don't deserve me"—a brute confidence that was necessary to get me through stage one. Stage two was missing the church— forgetting how toxic it had been, and maybe just feeling lonely and missing being in a relationship. I didn't want to go back to that church, but I missed being part of a community, I missed the sense of belonging that I'd had, and I missed my faith. But how could I miss something that had handed me heartbreak?

This is what high-stakes mistakes do to a person: They

throw you into a state of uncertainty and questioning your-self. Was I willing to risk acting in the same way that had gotten me hurt? Was I stupid to want to try the thing that hurt me again? Was it weird for me to want it? And perhaps the most important question: Would I be strong enough to heal if this happened again?

We all know this feeling. Can I trust again? Can I love again? Can I forgive them? Can I forgive myself?

Sometimes when we make a mistake and it costs us, we avoid making that same mistake again. I have a friend who hit a rock while riding their bike and took a spill over the handlebars and broke their collarbone. And guess what: They just decided never to get on a bike again, and that is a completely reasonable response. But I also have friends who have made mistakes in areas of life that cannot, and I believe should not, be avoided. I have friends who, in tan-dem with their own trauma, have cheated on their partners. Sitting with a friend who just made a mistake that blew up their entire life is an excruciating type of pain. Have you ever wanted so badly to tell someone that everything was going to be OK, but you were not sure it was true? And coming from the other end, it is not unusual to hear some-thing like "I don't deserve to be with anyone, so I'm just gonna be alone for the rest of my life to protect the people I love from myself." In a lot of ways, it's good to slow down after a high-stakes mistake and not jump from relationship to relationship. Slowing down can give us the space we need to process our own actions, the actions of others, and how the two interact. Slow is good, but we don't want to stop altogether.

When we make high-stakes mistakes that are socially charged—when we say something racist or homophobic, or when our high-stakes mistakes are aired for all to see—slowing down and taking a moment after that is a great thing to do, but stopping completely is far more common. I know a lot of people who have tried to enter a conversation, got called out for making a mistake, and never got back into the conversation after that. Don't let that be you.

High-stakes mistakes should not slow us all the way down, but they should make us pause. Researchers from NYU have actually found that our brains are wired for us to move more slowly after a mistake. We will take more time after a mistake. Makes sense, right? You cut your hand chopping garlic and the next time you cut garlic, you will move more slowly, more deliberately, with more attention. You go back to the shop to replace the coffee you left on the top of your car, and you are going to slow down and make sure everything is in its right place before you drive off. So how do we apply this to high-stakes mistakes?

In my opinion, most people trying to recover after making a high-risk mistake fall into one of two camps. The first camp is the group of people who choose to retreat.

Part of the problem is that to avoid making high-stakes mistakes, we can simply choose not to reach past what is certain and comfortable for us. Our brains know the risk, we have experienced heartbreak, we have been on the outside of the community, we have felt shame and guilt, and we simply refuse to go down that road again. I think we all know people who fall into this camp—and I'm certain that we have all fallen into it at some point. When my boyfriend in college cheated on me, I remember saying many times to several different people, "I'm just gonna stay single forever." It was safe, it was comfortable, and it allowed me to avoid being hurt again at that level. I was wrong once, I could be wrong again, and so I would just stay where I was. I thought the same thing after being forced outside of my church community, that I would never be a part of a church community again. I would just stay where I was, and opening myself up to a sense of belonging again was simply not worth the risk. I had made high-stakes mistakes. I trusted people who hurt me, and that would be the last time.

This is also how it can feel when we make big social and political mistakes. I have a friend from college who, around 2009, got a Kanye West tattoo on his arm. As his friends, we all felt it was a bold move, but I remember him telling us, "I don't think there is anything Kanye could ever do that would make me regret getting this tattoo." Well, here we are in 2024, and he regrets it. I am sure it was hard for people who voted for Trump in 2016 to turn around in 2020 and feel that they had made a high-stakes mistake. That is an extremely vulnerable feeling, and it can be easier to dig our heels even deeper in the sand and cling tight to the empty sense of security that can give us. It can make us feel safe, but it certainly is not helpful for where we want to go.

The other feeling that can come from experiencing the consequences of a high-stakes mistake is that you begin not only to shut down but also to become protective, like a snake that has coiled itself up, closed itself off, and simply rejected its new environment. This is the posture we see with all of the people right now who feel that they are "under attack": It is the posture of the comedians who feel they are being oppressed, silenced, and victimized in a culture that wants to see their demise, because, let's be honest, accountability can sting, and realizing that we have made high-stakes mistakes and that those mistakes have consequences can bring out our most primal response: self-protection. The narrative can shift quickly from "I need to take responsibility for my actions" to "This cancel culture is out to get me." But I can guarantee you that this response will not get us anywhere near where we want to be. This response will cause the pendulum to swing all the way back to where it was. Recently, the comedian, podcast host, and former *Fear Factor* host Joe Rogan opened an "anti-woke" comedy club in Austin, Texas. He describes it as a "safe space" for comedians. Well, I don't think that is the answer. How do we go from mistakes to something better, not back to something worse?

The second camp people fall into after making a high-risk mistake sucks. It's harder, messier, more dangerous. It asks a lot of us. It doesn't give us room to coil up, to protect.

It asks for risk, but it can give reward. The second camp is all about risk: risking to trust again, to forgive, to be open to changing our minds, to believe new realities—to forgive.

Once I had gone through my faith deconstruction and started the journey of reconstruction, I found myself back in a familiar situation. I was a pastor again. Only this time, instead of a room of people all trying to hide the truest parts of themselves and pretending to have right answers, I was now gifted with the opportunity to have deep and meaningful conversations with a community of people who were admittedly still trying to figure it all out. It is one of my favorite things that I get to do because it is one of the most honest spaces I occupy. But it's not easy. Most of the people who find themselves in that room have entered with lots of bags they are unpacking about what it means to be a person of faith, bags filled with traumatizing experiences, bags needing to be rearranged and their contents refolded. I love that part of it, but sometimes, in my quest to create conversation and connection, I unknowingly hit a land mine hidden amid the baggage of my community. A few years ago, I was preparing for a conversation about forgiveness. It felt like a fairly innocuous thing to bring up; after all, who doesn't like forgiveness? Around five minutes into my talk, I felt the entire mood of the room change. It was as if everyone began holding their breath and the air in the room went as stiff as the people's backs against their chairs—they seemed desperate for me to talk about literally anything else.

One of my favorite things about our church is that

we spend a lot of time on Sundays having conversations, and after the sermon there's a big group discussion where folks in the room share their feelings about what was talked about, or comments they have, new things to add to the conversation—it's the best part of who we are. Well, after my sermon on this particular day, the conversation was intense. As soon as the gates were open, I was flooded with stories of how the word *forgiveness* and the concept of it had been weaponized and used to put people in our community in compromising, harmful, and abusive situations. Many folks shared about being forced to "forgive" someone who hurt them, and in this context, forgiveness essentially meant just letting it go. There were countless stories with the same sentiment: Someone got hurt and then a pastor, church leader, or parent said to them, "You need to forgive," and then after that moment of "forgiveness," the thing that hurt them was never able to be addressed again.

Does this sound familiar to you? Whether or not you grew up in the church, I think a lot of us have experienced this diluted and oppressive concept of forgiveness. Forgiveness is what you do when you are ready to move on and never look back? Or forgiveness is just something you say to a person who hurt you? I hate how we talk about forgiveness, because I think it is actually one of the most life-giving experiences we can offer ourselves and those around us, but we need a deeper understanding. We need to understand the groundbreaking experience of what true forgiveness can offer us, and then we need to put it into practice.

Forgiveness is not a single moment; it's not the moment when your brother takes something from you and your mom makes him reluctantly apologize, and then you say you forgive him, but really this is just another blip on the radar of your sibling relationship, endlessly annoying each other until someone cries. But that's the picture we get of forgiveness, right? Someone hurts us, says they are sorry, and we forgive them. Or the harder one: Someone hurts us, never apologizes, and we still have to find a way to forgive them. In any case, we position forgiveness as a singular moment, as the moment we have to release the weight of whatever hurt or harm we have held. But I don't think forgiveness is a moment; I think it's active, ongoing.

A big part of forgiveness is what is happening and continues to happen in us when we are able to enter back into situations that were the places or settings that caused us harm. It's all of the people sitting in our church after a church was the setting where they were hurt—it doesn't have anything to do with them going back to the people and place that hurt them; instead, it's about being open to church again. It's forgiveness. Even with suspicion and moving slowly, it's forgiveness. It's the part of us that is willing to believe that just because one thing hurts, that does not mean all things will. Forgiveness is my wife being open to loving me and being in a relationship with me even though she had been hurt in relationships. Forgiveness is me allowing myself to be a pastor even after I lived a life where that role did what I now believe was harm. Forgiveness is the way we see everything around us, including ourselves.

The second camp is forgiveness after mistakes; it is openness to a new reality. Sometimes, to get there, we need to understand the reality of what happened; we need to understand the lived and required consequences, and experience accountability. Only after that can we start to forgive.

6

Accountability, Not Annihilation

WHEN I WAS IN EIGHTH GRADE, I DID SOMETHING STUPID.
Not only was it stupid, it was also completely pre-
meditated and planned. It was an intentionally stupid
moment. Middle school was the time I was really starting to
discover my sense of humor. I started developing a reputation for being funny, and that title meant everything to me,
so I knew that before I left middle school, I had to go out
with a bang. I had to leave my comedy mark on this school,
forever and always. Because I was just starting to realize
that I might have the potential to be funny, I wasn't starting
out with stand-up sets in the cafeteria; instead, a lot of my
humor was working itself through the vehicle of pranks. I
was a nonstop prank train, and I can't even imagine how
annoying that was for everyone around me. But when I

sat back and thought about how to leave my mark on the school and cement myself in the middle school prankster hall of fame, I was gifted with an idea while watching one of the greatest movies of all time. There is a scene in *Sister Act 2: Back in the Habit* where the students want to show their disapproval for Whoopi Goldberg as their new music teacher, so they come together and decide to glue her to the chair. In the movie, this scene is iconic. Whoopi realizes she is glued to the chair; she gives a slight scowl and rolls herself out of the room using the wheels on her chair as the class erupts into not only laughter but also spontaneous song—it's incredible. A lightbulb went off in my very underdeveloped, thirteen-year-old brain. *That's it! That is how I will leave my comedy mark on this place: I am going to glue my teacher to the chair.*

I made all the appropriate arrangements. I had a friend who was into making models, and he gave me a half-full tube of airplane modeling glue. I made up a reason I had to be at school early, and I arrived before the teacher or my classmates. I ran into the room, lathered the chair with as much sticky, coagulated modeling glue as I could squeeze out of the tube, and then went into the hallway to await my friends with giddy anticipation. I could not wait to tell them that I actually went through with it, I pulled it off, and it was going to be absolutely hilarious. Of course, in my mind, it was going to go exactly how it went in the movie. Our teacher would realize he was stuck to the chair, he would have a confused, slightly angry look on his face, and then the whole class would erupt into laughter and maybe even

song. The possibilities felt endless, and all I knew for sure
was that this was going to be one of the best days of my life.

As the class began, I could barely sit down, I was filled
with so much anticipation. At our middle school, the first
period of each day began with a ten-minute "news show"
that was produced by students. It was cute, but it meant that
when our teacher came into the room, he sat on the chair
and remained seated for ten minutes while we watched
this student-produced news and announcement segment. I
couldn't believe it—it was actually happening; he was really
sitting down in a lot of modeling glue. What would happen
next? I could not even bring myself to focus long enough to
hear a single word of the news and announcements. The
morning show ended. Here it was, the big moment. What
song would our class spontaneously erupt into? How hard
would everyone be laughing? Would they spit water out of
their noses? Would they hoist my desk and seat into the air
while they chanted my name? How would this legendary
moment in my comedy career play out? My cheeks were
red. I was ready for my moment.

Just as I suspected, the morning show ended, and our
teacher went to stand up out of his chair, and it happened.
The chair came with him. They were a package deal.
Teacher and chair together like peanut butter and jelly. I
waited for the laughs, but there was nothing. Silence. My
excitement quickly started to turn to something else; I
didn't know what else yet, but not excitement. The silly look
of whimsical confusion I imagined would be on our teacher's face was nothing like the look Whoopi Goldberg had

on hers. He wiggled the chair a bit, and he slowly became angrier and angrier, until finally, he pushed down with all of his might while uttering a loud and aggressive "What the *fuck?*" That was the moment I knew this was not going to go how I'd imagined. No one was erupting into song, and even worse, no one was laughing, not even a chuckle. It was bad. The chair did come off when he let out his blurt of profanity, but the modeling glue, in all of its glory, did take a chunk of his pants with it. This was not good. This was not funny. I was going to be in big trouble. My once-red cheeks, filled with giddy anticipation, were now ghost white as we watched our teacher storm out of the room with a piece of his Dockers still attached to the chair. The room was stunned. Half of our class had no idea what had just happened, and the other half knew exactly what had happened. I don't think in the history of eighth graders a room has ever been as quiet as that one was in that moment. The only thing that broke the silence was one of my friends leaning over to me to whisper, "You're screwed."

They were right. Later that afternoon, I was called into the dean's office. The dean held up a list of twenty or thirty names, and he simply said, "Here are all of the eighth graders who have confirmed it was you who glued Mr. Smith to his chair."

Immediately I regretted bragging to literally anyone who would listen about my plan. "What's gonna happen to me?" I asked.

The dean replied, "First, we are going to call your parents."

The whole thing was awful. They called my mom,

who called my dad, who left work to come and pick me up because the school said I had to leave immediately. I sat in the car with my dad, and we drove home in complete silence. It wasn't as silent as twenty eighth graders who had just heard their teacher say the F-word, but it was close. As we pulled into the driveway, the words spilled from his mouth: "What were you thinking?"

We waited patiently to hear from the school about what my punishment would be. They called and told my parents I would be suspended for three weeks and that I would have to pay to buy my teacher a new pair of pants. OK, that seemed fair, right? But my mom wasn't having it. She started arguing, "So you mean to tell me she gets a three-week vacation at home for breaking the rules? I don't think so." My mom argued with the lady on the phone until she caved and changed my punishment from an out-of-school suspension to an in-school suspension, which meant that instead of watching TV at home, I would be in a solo cubicle at school all day. Well played, Mom. The punishment ran its course, and I did chores for my neighbors to make money for the pants. The total was $42, and for a long time I kept the Kohl's receipt that he provided for the reimbursement. It felt important for some reason.

There are a lot of things I learned from that experience. (Honestly, probably not as many as I should have.) One thing that always stuck out to me was how the school decided on one punishment and my mom made them change it. I thought that places like school and work just decide something for you and you can't change it. But in this scenario, my mom was not satisfied with their consequences, and not only did she make the school change them, but she also added her own. I felt bad enough that I felt I deserved everything coming my way, and I was happy to be dusting my neighbors' house so that my teacher could have new pants. But I was thirteen, and my parents and my school were the sole voices of consequences and punishments in my life. Every time I stepped out of line (which was often), I would await their response. Sometimes I would carry out my consequences dutifully and fairly, and sometimes I would feel they were unfair, and I would make my way through them. I felt bad about gluing my teacher to the chair, the consequences felt fair, and I was happy to participate in them.

But I did other things and suffered other consequences and punishments that I didn't think were fair. I remember one time we got caught toilet papering someone's house. To be clear, this particular someone had said something mean to my friend, so covering the trees outside of her house in toilet paper felt like a completely appropriate response. I think I was grounded for a week, but I was not happy about it—I did not think I deserved it: I felt very justified in my choice to whimsically launch rolls of Charmin into pine trees as a punishment for her comments about my friend. But whatever; I took the punishment and checked the box because I was thirteen and I had no choice. But what do we do when we grow up and we do have a choice?

Who gets to hand out the consequences and punishments? Does it matter if we feel remorse or not as long as we serve our time? Does it matter if we knew what we were doing was wrong?

These are the questions I have while watching online celebrity figures fumble their way through the apology videos they make for stupid ideas that they had . . . and acted on. Did they think these ideas would be funny? The more public Instagram apologies I watch, the more I am reminded of what it feels like to have an idea that you think will have people laughing so hard that water comes out of their nose, an idea so good it may have people chanting your name, an idea you believe will be your greatest moment, and then having it turn into regret and remorse, leaving you sitting silently in a car with your dad, awaiting the consequences.

Is that how comedians feel? Is that why Joe Rogan is opening an anti-woke comedy club? Did he think his peers would burst into spontaneous song when he told his jokes about women, but instead they turned on him? Is he turning his rejection into blame to avoid his consequences? Sometimes I think that's how my friend Rachel felt. Maybe she recorded that video thinking, "This is great content, people will love it," but not long after that, she found herself sitting silently in her home awaiting the consequences. Running back through her brain, wondering how she did not put these pieces together sooner. I don't remember my teenage brain ever thinking, "Hey, this is kind of a mean thing to do to a person. What if no one thinks it's funny?" Now that I am probably the age that my teacher was at the time I glued him to the chair, I can't imagine this happening to me. Is that the same kind of emotional blindness that influencers who say stupid things feel? They were reaching for a quick laugh, and the room turned on them. Is that how people who voted for Trump in 2016 felt when it seemed like a good idea at the time? Is that how that seventeen-year-old kid Diego felt when he got drunk and shared that picture? A lot of people make a lot of mistakes, and sometimes we start out the mistakes thinking they are actually good ideas. I get it. I've been there. So what next? Who gets the money for the new pants? Who decides what consequences and punishments will be sufficient for us to allow them back on our screens?

What do we do with a public apology that feels genuine and remorseful? What do we do with the ones that feel robotic and mechanical?

What is our goal in handing out societal consequences and social punishments?

What's difficult about a lot of these situations is that no one has been in the same exact scenario, so a lot of us speculate about what we would do, what should be done, and also what should have been done.

Have you ever noticed that no one has more ideas and advice about parenting than people without kids? The internet is riddled with them. Ashamedly, I can remember a time or two when I have given advice that, looking back, was so obviously based on no information or experience that it is wildly embarrassing. One of my very new parent friends was complaining about how tired they were, how they were waking up every hour all night, how they couldn't function throughout the day, how they were fighting now because they were just so tired. So many of the problems they were sharing all seemed to hinge on their exhaustion, so being the brilliant problem solver that I am, I suggested a very clear solution: "Why don't you just teach your baby how to sleep through the night?"

My wife and I made the decision a few years ago that we were not going to have kids, and since then, we have become a major minority in our friend group. Probably 95 percent of our friends have kids, and it has been fascinating to watch so many people we love navigate this new frontier of parenthood.

The endless questions that come up when you are trying to teach someone how to be a human in the world. How to respond when their kids inevitably and pretty regularly do things they aren't supposed to be doing, or when they do dangerous things that can hurt them, or just plain naughty things because they are kids. What do you do when your kid does something they aren't supposed to do? When they bite their brother or kick a kid at recess or don't like the taste of chicken anymore and throw the bowl of chicken onto the floor? How do you wrap your head around how two people, the same people, can have multiple children who are all wildly different and require different kinds of parenting? I think we have a lot to learn from parents and the realities of parenting. Beyond raising kind people who are also hopefully not picky eaters (my irrational nonnegotiable), I think parenting has a lot to teach us about how we respond to ourselves and the other adults around us who are still very much trying to figure out how to be human.

Like a lot of people during the pandemic, I spent far too many hours scrolling TikTok, and for the most part, TikTok knew me. The algorithm understood what I wanted—it was serving me endless videos of new recipes, lesbians, cute dogs, and cars being detailed. Judge me if you want, but I live for watching an old Toyota Tacoma go through a *Miss Congeniality*-level transformation. But there were a few things the TikTok algorithm did not understand about me. For starters, TikTok was very convinced that I speak Spanish, probably because whenever videos in Spanish came on, I would watch them and try to see how much of it I understood (very little). But also somehow I ended up on the "gentle parenting" side of TikTok. A lot of the videos would be sharing a situation and taking an approach that most of us who are over the age of thirty did not experience as children. One of the first gentle parenting videos I saw was of a kid who bit their mom. What I would imagine in that scenario is the parent just very sternly and seriously telling the kid to stop biting them, and maybe throwing a punishment in there too, like "If you bite me again, no more iPad." But in gentle parenting, it's different. This parent sat down with their kid and explained why they didn't like being bitten, explained that it hurt them, and also told their kid that they understood why they might want to bite something, and maybe they feel as though they need to bite something to feel good. The video ended with something like "Please do not bite Mommy, but if you need to bite something, tell me and we can go find something for you to bite." The next scene was the kid chomping down on a teething toy. You get the idea, right? Instead of demanding your kid stop throwing a tantrum in the middle of Target, you get down on the ground with them and say, "I know what it's like to have big feelings," or something very humanizing like that; that is gentle parenting.

I got so invested in watching these videos, they were so sweet, and then I started to see people who would record themselves watching gentle parenting videos, and there would be fully grown adults crying and talking about how this is helping them heal their inner child. So much beauty coming from these videos made me want to learn more about gentle parenting. As a person who doesn't have kids and isn't planning on having kids, these videos started to break something open in me. There was a lot for me to learn from these videos, and I think there is a lot for all of us to learn.

I started doing a little more research on gentle parenting and found that this parenting style is composed of four main elements—empathy, respect, understanding, and boundaries. With gentle parenting, you encourage the qualities you want in your child by being compassionate while simultaneously enforcing consistent boundaries. That sounds like exactly what we need in our adult world today.

Gentle parenting has a strong focus on a child's cognitive state, and parents use that state to establish guidelines and boundaries. The boundaries are all age-appropriate and beneficial to the child's development. Gentle parenting is an approach that focuses on fostering positive traits that are specific and unique to each child. Gentle parents (which is such a great name for what we should all be) model the behavior they expect to see from their children; gone are the days of "do as I say, not as I do." Because if it's not possible for you, you shouldn't expect it from others, right? Especially kids. While gentle parents discipline their children, the goal is to teach the child rather than to punish them for their behavior. Any discipline is shaped to help children better understand how they should behave and to understand the options that they have for responding to different situations, and the goal is to discipline the child without exposing them to any parent-led harm—no yelling, insulting, shaming. Sounds pretty great, right? Not only does gentle parenting provide a nice framework for imaginary kids I am not going to have, it has helped me put words, language, and a conceptual model around a question that I have had for a long time: that of the difference between consequences and punishments. Is there a way to address bad behavior without shame or punishments that also sets boundaries and makes space for consequences?

I realize that dealing with a toddler whom you are raising is quite different from dealing with a racist celebrity or a disappointing family member, but I also think there is a lot for us to learn from the parents who are pioneering the work that we so desperately want to see happen around us: A vision of human relationships where we pay attention to context, set boundaries, and expect only realistic change based on development and education. Where behaviors change because of understanding and not because of shame. Where actions have consequences, but people aren't punished for being who they are.

I was astonished at the restraint these parents exercised in the gentle parenting videos. A mother was just bitten, and she is kneeling on the floor asking a toddler if they want help picking out something that is more appropriate to bite? Now, I can't be certain, but I'm pretty sure gentle parenting would be the hardest thing. But it mirrors an experience I have had a lot, where I have been, or witnessed another person being, a victim of someone's poor ideology or theology or just plain bad behavior, and I really have to ask myself what I want to see from the person who caused the harm. What is the outcome I want for them?

When I was in my twenties and was a pastor at a very different kind of church from the one I am at now, I worked for a very specific kind of man. He was the head pastor, he was very charismatic, and he was able to make everyone feel as if he was their friend, which is a great trait to have when you are trying to build a megachurch. One thing that this man and the church participated in was particularly traumatizing to me. My old boss and his church found a way to never really be clear on where they stood on certain questions. If you went to this church, you could sort of read between the lines to find whatever you were looking for. Want to believe this church is a safe place for queer folks? There's a way you could read between the lines and find that. Does this church believe in the equality of women? Sure, if you look hard enough, you could probably find that. Even if you wanted the exact opposite—this isn't one of those churches that lets gay people in, right? Yeah, you could find that too. We don't support women leading men here, right? Yep, you could find that. This church was an absolute master class in riding the line. And sure, I guess to get thousands of people to go to your church in Los Angeles, you've got to ride the line, and never say anything too extreme one way or another, and hope that the full band, the lights, and the fog machines will distract everyone from looking too hard, and so far it has worked out for him.

Of course, I worked for him and was on the receiving end of finding out the hard way exactly where he stood. In my view, there is no doubt in his mind that queer folks are not living the way his specific god intended, and I think he was also very clear that he did not believe women could be in the highest level of leadership at the church. Needless to say, it really bothers me that this man is just continuing to publicly ride a line that he privately has fully built a home on one side of. I feel so bothered when I think about how much I have sacrificed, the public criticism I have been subjected to, the private messages I have received, the price I have paid for being open and honest about where I stand. And don't get me wrong: I would do it all again in a heartbeat, because nothing compares to being true to who I am. But I do have one hypothetical scenario that drives me absolutely mad. I sometimes ask myself what I would do, how I would feel, if one day my old boss came out publicly standing for all of the things that I stand for now. What if he has privately undergone some sort of massive life transformation and now believes queer people are good and worthy people, and he has rejected his previously held patriarchal idea of power and leadership and become an advocate and ally of women? I genuinely believe that him doing this or saying and believing these things publicly would get him a lot of praise, and that infuriates me.

Why? Why would it make me mad that someone changed? Transformed? Became more evolved and inclusive in their ideology? Because that's what I want, ultimately, but I also want him to have to get it the hard way. I want it to be a painful process for him because it was a painful process for me. The idea that he could go from Mr. Riding the Line to Mr. Hero the Ally bothers me. I want him to be exposed for who he is now, before he changes his mind, and then I want him to go through consequences. I want him to be punished for what he believed, and I want him to feel bad about it—and *then* I want him to change his mind. And that's how I know I still have my own work to do. I don't want anybody to gentle parent this man; I want public shame. If I were his parent and he threw a fit in Target, I would be the parent who threw a tantrum in his classroom the next day just to prove a point. You embarrassed me, so I'll embarrass you.

Have you ever had these feelings? Does any of that feel familiar? I get it, I feel it too, and I understand how, for a lot of us who don't have access to the people who hurt us, we join in on the public flogging of an obscure internet person because we just want someone to feel what we have felt in some way. That is human, and it makes sense, but it also might be something we need to examine. It might be where we need to gentle parent ourselves first. Because I don't want a world of retribution; I want transformation.

What is the difference between wanting someone to have consequences and accountability for bad behavior and wanting someone to experience harm because they caused harm? How can we know which one we are fighting for?

Most of us know what retaliation looks like; we know that embarrassing our kids because they embarrassed us in Target may not be the best way to raise responsible kids. But when we watch people in our lives swing big and miss, make mistakes, embarrass us—what do we want in return?

I'll be the first one to admit that I do not hate when bad things happen to bad people. You all now know how I feel about my old boss and pastor. I also love that people are experiencing real consequences for saying racist things on the internet. I don't want a complete loosey-goosey world where people run around harming each other and there are no boundaries and no consequences, but I am asking if the road we are charting leads to transformation, to growth, or to shame and guilt. And before you ask—no, I do not have the exact plans for that road. But I can tell you that a lot of what I see looks like throwing tantrums in someone's space because someone threw a tantrum in yours, and I just don't think that is going to end well. A celebrity said something racist and lost their brand deals? Great, that's the consequence now. What is the road to them being less racist? A comedian made a transphobic joke and got their comedy special taken down? Fantastic. Now what's the road to them not being transphobic? I'm here for the consequences, I think they are how we set boundaries with adults, but after the consequences, is it possible not to double down on the punishments, to stop the frenzy and offer something else? Something deeper? Something new?

I believe in the core of who I am that transformation is always the goal, that growth is possible, and that people can find, share, and create spaces for healing. Yet I am constantly challenged when I think about what that core belief means for me with regard to accountability. I ask myself this often, particularly when I am following the discourse online.

Back to TikTok, there was a young woman I followed who had a pretty massive platform—in the millions. She was a college basketball player, and over the course of her public life on TikTok, she had a girlfriend who also had millions of followers. The couple built an even stronger platform together, and then sadly, they broke up, because that's what happens to a good portion of relationships in college. Rumors circulated that this basketball player turned social media star had cheated on her girlfriend, and what happened next was heartbreaking to watch. In her senior year and her last season of basketball, she suffered a career-ending injury. She made a tearful video about the whole ordeal, and the comments were shocking. I stopped scrolling after probably the first hundred, but they all went something to the effect of "This is what you get," and "You deserve this," and "Looks like karma is working." It was bonkers. Why did so many people feel this was an appropriate punishment for her? Why were adults in her comments acting like feral children saying some of the most unnecessarily hateful things I've ever read? Because she broke up with someone?

My friend Rachel, who I talked about earlier, said wildly inappropriate things on the internet, and as a result, there were consequences. She lost followers, brand deals, partnerships. OK, I like consequences; I think consequences are good and healthy and helpful. But punishments? I don't think those have a helpful role to play in the story of how we become better people. The consequences happened, and there are people in her comments and life who still want more. They don't feel the consequences are enough, and they want her to hurt, they want her to feel ashamed, they want a constant and total reminder that she caused harm, and I understand that feeling. I have been there; I have people in my life who can take me back there, but that is not where I want to live, want to stay, and it's not a place that can take us anywhere but down.

This conversation makes a lot more sense if we are talking about parenting, or even if we are talking about small mistakes, but what do we do with people who mess up in a big way? Publicly?

I have always been a pretty idealistic person; I have lived a lot of my life in the clouds of "how things could be." My brother, on the other hand, lives his life pretty firmly planted in what is. Earlier in his career, when he was a young professional and I was an extremely idealistic nineteen-year-old, my brother worked inside of a prison, and one day we got into an argument. I had read approximately one third of a book about prison reform, and that was enough for me to tell my brother that prisons shouldn't exist, that they are a punishment that doesn't bring transformation, that they are modern-day slavery . . . I went on and on. I talked about what happens when we dehumanize people the way prison does, and so on. We argued for a while before my brother just said, "OK, why don't you come to work with me and see for yourself?" Now, at no point in my life had I ever been to prison, but armed with minimal knowledge (an unfortunate yet constant theme in my life), I went to work with my brother.

It was not what I had imagined. I was yelled at and reached for in ways that terrified me. I found my mind absolutely bouncing back and forth between wanting to abolish prisons and being grateful for these bars between me and the prisoners. It was an awful day and an experience I am eternally grateful for. Since that day, I have not changed one thing that I think or believe about prisons and the damage they do; I have not wavered in my thoughts and beliefs and understanding of the people inside them. If anything, I have doubled down. I left the prison that day and finished that book, got more books, and had more conversations, but what I knew after that trip that I didn't know before was that my ideals could be as clean and clear as I could make them, but ideals and hopes always meet somewhere with the messy reality that we are all just human. I still believe what I have always believed about prison, but I'm not naïve enough to think it's not complicated. I want a path forward for humanity; I want people who make mistakes to be able to come back and transform. I believe that with every part of me, but let's not pretend it's not complicated; *we* are complicated.

We need boundaries, we need consequences for our actions, but I think the question we need to be desperately asking is how we can sit in the murky waters of what it means to allow room for transformation after consequences. How can we hold back punishment? What empathy needs to be extended to ourselves so it can also be extended to others? I think we have to be willing to get into the real world, to walk into the places we have lots of big ideas about. Get out of comment sections and into the conversations happening at the dinner tables around us. There is no rule book, no manual that tells us "this homophobic remark equals this consequence." We are figuring all of this out in real time, and it's hard. It's messy, it's painful, and it is so wildly important.

What do we do with people who fuck up in a big way? Big consequences.

7

Boundaries to the Rescue

J UST SO WE ARE CLEAR, I BELIEVE IN THE POTENTIAL IN ALL people, and I want healing and transformation and the kind of accountability that can make a way to new behavior, but I also am a person who is angry and has moods and swings with the winds of the world.

When I was in college and really starting to understand my racial and ethnic identity in a new way, I was presented with an opportunity to learn something that has been stamped in my brain ever since. It was a moment and experience that allowed me to better understand what was happening not only in the world around me but also, more importantly, in me. It happened one Thursday night. One of the administrators, who was also one of my mentors in college, came to one of the weekly meetings

that the Black student group held in the lobby of a dor-
mitory. She brought along her husband that night, and
both of them taught us something I had never had the
opportunity to learn before: racial identity development
theory. It was a fun and interactive night. They used us all
as human props for building a conceptual model, and they
also brought free pizza. I spent that Thursday night in the
lobby learning something that I would take with me into
every season I've had since.

The model they taught us was created by Dr. Derald
Wing Sue and Dr. David Sue. They are both professors,
and brothers, who research and teach identity development. Dr. Derald Wing Sue is actually one of the most cited
multicultural scholars in the United States.

Drs. Sue and Sue's model for understanding racial and
cultural identity development is one that I have always
found extremely helpful, not only in deepening understanding of my own experience but also helping me better
understand and have language for where the people around
me might also find themselves. The model is relatively simple; it outlines five stages for BIPOC folks and seven stages
for white folks. I know that this would probably be more
fun if we were all in a room and I was using you as props,
and also if I had free pizza, but nevertheless, I want to share
this model with you because I think it holds a lens that can
help us understand how we enter the murky gray waters of
human relationships that we are all trying to navigate. As
we go through these stages, we will take only a brief look at
a complex idea, but it is important for us to get a snapshot

of how this works. So while you may not leave this chapter with a doctorate in identity development, let's do our best to wrap our heads around some basics.

First, let's take a look at the five stages for **BIPOC** folks.

The first stage is *conformity*. This stage is one that I understand well from my experiences growing up in predominantly white environments. This is the stage where someone has positive attitudes toward and even a preference for dominant cultural values that, in our context, are rooted in whiteness. This is also the stage where individuals place considerable value on characteristics that represent dominant cultural groups. In this stage, someone might even devalue or hold negative views of their own race or other racial/ethnic groups that are not part of the dominant white culture. Essentially, in this stage, folks prefer whiteness and see whiteness as the aspirational standard. This was my experience in middle school when I wanted to straighten my hair so that it looked like the other girls' at my school. Now, there's nothing wrong with straight hair, but I didn't want it because I liked it; I wanted it so I could be closer to whiteness. That is the desire in this stage—you want to conform to the standard that has been presented to you and to most Americans. We live in a culture that presents whiteness as the standard. I think we can all either think about a time when we felt this, or at least we can think of a celebrity who finds themselves in this stage.

The second stage is *dissonance and appreciating*. This is the stage when someone begins to question identity. This is where you might start to recognize conflicting messages or

observe problems, become aware of something that challenges your beliefs, and start to question the value you have
put on mainstream cultural groups. This is where you begin
to develop a growing sense of your own cultural heritage.
In this stage, you also become more aware of the existence
of racism and start to move away from seeing dominant
cultural groups as all good. For me, the experience I can
most closely understand coming into this stage was in high
school when, for the first time, I read *The Autobiography of
Malcolm X* and started to wonder why I didn't like my natural hair. It's when I started to wonder whether whiteness
was the thing I should be aspiring to when it was the thing
that was producing so much harm in the world and in my
own life experience. This is the stage for those questions to
begin to bloom.

The third stage is *resistance and immersion*. In this stage,
you begin to embrace and hold positive attitudes toward
and preferences for your own race. This experience will also
cause you to reject dominant values of society and culture;
you stop seeing whiteness as the best standard and goal,
and instead you turn your focus to eliminating oppression
within your own racial/cultural group. This stage brings
with it big feelings. These feelings could look like distrust
and anger—toward the white dominant cultural groups
and anything that may represent them. This stage has a big
shift where you begin to place considerable value on characteristics that represent your own cultural groups without
question, and you develop a growing appreciation for others
from racially and culturally diverse groups. So, if you are

Black, this stage could be where you not only start reject-ing whiteness but also begin valuing the Latinx experience or the AAPI experience along with the foremost apprecia-tion going to your own racial and cultural group. For me, after I read *The Autobiography of Malcolm X*, I started reading everything I could get my hands on related to the Black Power movement, the Black Panther Party, Fred Hampton, Huey P. Newton, and Marcus Garvey. These books led me to other books by and about radical leaders, and I began to devour all things Black and disdain all things white.

OK, are you still with me? I know we are deep in this, but understanding these stages and our movement through them is going to set us up so well for understanding how to set and assess boundaries within ourselves and the people around us, so let's keep going.

The fourth stage is *introspection*. This is where you begin to question the psychological cost of projecting strong feel-ings toward dominant cultural groups; you desire to focus more energy on personal identity while respecting your own cultural groups. It is hard to be angry all the time, and this is where you start to feel that and begin to look for something else. You realign your perspective to note that not all aspects of dominant cultural groups—one's own racial/cultural group or other diverse groups—are good or bad; this may cause a struggle and cause you to experience conflicts of loy-alty as your perspective broadens. This is the stage where the binary breaks down and you feel conflicted. I have had this experience many times where I begin to let go of the anger, to have a broader perspective, and sometimes I have a voice in the back of my head (and voices online) telling me that I am not radical enough, that broadening my perspective to include white people, to not categorize people as "all good" or "all bad," isn't a strong enough position to allow me to stay in some of the groups I have found myself in. This is the stage that reflects some of the things we were talking about earlier—this is the stage where you start to discover what you need to move forward, but you have to hold it in tandem with the perception it might give people of you. It challenges our blind followership ideals and begins to put the mirror back on ourselves and what we need to thrive. James Baldwin once said, "To be a Negro in this country and to be relatively conscious is to be in a rage almost, almost all of the time." And I believe that it is true—and in this stage, you begin to ask or imagine another way past the constant rage. Is there more? Is there another way?

The fifth and final stage for BIPOC folks is *integrative awareness.* This is the stage in which you have developed a secure, confident sense of racial/cultural identity and you become multicultural. You maintain pride in your own racial identity and cultural heritage, you commit to supporting and appreciating all oppressed and diverse groups, and you tend to recognize racism as a societal illness by which all can be victimized. This stage is where I have found myself a time or two. This is the stage I think I feel at my most integrated self, but I will be very honest in saying that I have not always stayed here.

Here is the absolute most important thing to know about these stages: They are not linear.

You do not graduate from one stage to another and then stay there. You move through these again and again as the culture shifts, as relationships shift, as life happens. Maybe I'm sitting in integrative awareness and feeling hopeful and secure in who I am, but what do you think happens when I open Instagram to find hundreds of people reposting a video of an unarmed Black man being murdered for being Black? You think I stay in this secure posture? Or do you think it makes sense that I would go right back to stage two and it's us versus them? What happens when I am in a state of introspecting, wondering how sustainable it is to hold this much rage and thinking about how I could hold hope as well, and then some random lady in the store makes a comment about my hair? Back to rage.

Understanding our identity development as fluid is not only incredibly freeing but also absolutely necessary if we are going to understand how to set, hold, and assess boundaries.

Before we get too far, let me tell you about the stages that white folks go through, and then we can talk about what to do next.

So for my white friends, a lot of the stages are similar but there is some variance and nuance that is specific, so there are seven stages. The first stage is *naïveté*. In this stage, you may have an early childhood developmental phase of curiosity or minimal awareness of race. The significance of race and culture has not yet been made apparent to your life and understanding. Depending on your specific experience, you may or may not receive specific and overt messages about other racial groups, but overall you possess an ethnocentric view of culture, meaning whiteness is all you see and/or understand. This is the stage a lot of my friends were in during high school when they would ask me what I "was," and when I would return the question they would say something like "I'm just normal white." In this stage people do not think or notice a lot about the world around them in regard to race. In this stage, you see yourself as just "normal," and you assume everyone else does too.

The second stage is *conformity*. This is where you have minimal awareness of yourself as a racial person. You believe strongly in the universality of values and norms. You perceive white American cultural groups as more highly developed, and you may justify the disparity of treatment other groups receive. You could be unaware of beliefs that reflect this—this message is so ingrained in you during this stage that you don't realize it's not universal, that it is just something you have come to believe. I think we are all aware of this stage. This is "American over everything," but in this stage, "American" is synonymous with "white," and because of that, if America is the best, then white is better too. (Side note: Sometimes when we talk about white supremacy, we have an idea in our head of neo-Nazis marching in the streets, but what we don't always think about or even notice are the ways in which we have associated whiteness with America and then valued America as superior.) In this stage, these wheels have not yet started turning and you are unaware of these connections; you just see yourself as someone who has traditional American morals and values.

Third is *dissonance*. This is when you experience an opportunity to examine your own prejudices and biases. You begin to move toward the realization that the dominant society oppresses racially and culturally diverse groups. This stage can often bring up feelings of shame, anger, and depression about the perpetuation of racism by white American cultural groups. From here, this stage can go one of two ways: You might begin to question previously held beliefs or, out of the discomfort, you refortify prior views and find yourself back in the second stage (remember, these are not linear). This is the stage that we saw a lot of white people collectively get to in 2020. We saw the dissonance of realizing that innocent Black lives were being taken, that racism and oppression were, in fact, far more prevalent than they ever realized, and I believe if we search our minds, we can find examples of the friends we know who let this dissonance push them to question previously held beliefs. I am sure we can also think of the people who, when faced with too much dissonance, doubled down on previous ideas to avoid this feeling. This stage is certainly a turning point.

The fourth stage is *resistance and immersion*. Past the dissonance, as you continue to question your previously held beliefs and as you face the real and present threat of racism and oppression in the world, you find yourself here, in immersion. In immersion, you begin to experience increased awareness of your own racism and how racism is projected in society. You start to see racism in the media, in movies, in books, in your family. You will likely feel angry about messages concerning other racial and cultural groups and guilty for being part of an oppressive system. Your eyes are open, and you are feeling angry. In this stage, you might try to counteract these feelings by assuming a paternalistic role and assuming you know what is best for the groups you are wanting to help, or you might find yourself over-identifying with another racial/cultural group. This is the stage that was very present online during the summer of 2020. There was a lot of resistance to whiteness, and you saw white people want to separate themselves from white-ness in any way they could; maybe it was their knowledge of racism and their attacking of other white people; maybe it was a distant indigenous heritage; maybe it was a queer identity. This is the stage when you want to be anything but "just white."

Fifth, *introspection*. This is where you begin to redefine what it means to be a white American and to be a racial and cultural being. This is the stage in which you begin to recognize your inability to fully understand the experience of others from diverse racial and cultural backgrounds, and you may also feel disconnected from the white American group. In this stage, it becomes more about who you are and less about proving to others who you aren't.

Sixth is *integrative awareness*. In this stage you can appreci-ate racial, ethnic, and cultural diversity; you become aware of and understand yourself as a racial and cultural being. This is where you become aware of the sociopolitical influ-ences of racism and you begin to internalize, for yourself, a nonracist identity. This is the place where things turn even more back to you, and you find a sense of security in who you are. You understand the social position that you hold, and you begin to hold an identity that is nonracist.

The final stage for my white friends is *commitment to antiracist action*. This is where you commit to social action to eliminate oppression and racism. This may look like vocalizing objections to racist jokes, taking steps to eradicate racism in institutions and systems you are a part of, or advocating for public policies. Unlike previous stages, you are not doing this for perception or performance. In this stage, you will likely feel pressure from your dominant group to go back to conformity. When we talk about "doing the work," this is the result that we have in our minds—we have a community of white folks who have a secure and committed identity that holds a commitment to antiracist action. But remember, these stages are not linear, so even if you have a season in this stage or find yourself here on occasion, once you make it here, you are not here to stay. You haven't "graduated." You can still experience conversations and moments of relationships that will have you float to another stage. There can be moments at work when confronting a racist joke feels like second nature, but you freeze and laugh along with the joke made by your uncle at the Thanksgiving table.

If we look back to our conversation about comedians, I think a lot of them, especially in 2020, wanted to be here. They wanted to be people who fight against racism—who *wants* to be racist? But as they looked around, maybe they felt that now they were the butt of the joke, that they were experiencing some sort of perceived oppression. Their own journey toward antiracism probably never made it past that dissonance, and we find ourselves with white comedians creating "safe spaces" for themselves because they feel under attack. Maybe it's not even that extreme. Maybe it just feels too overwhelming; maybe you feel as though you have been doing the work, but no progress is being made. Maybe you felt a sense of urgency and a rush to make change in 2020, but then you had kids, you moved out of the city, and your commitment to antiracism slowly faded back to conformity.

I am not saying this to shame anyone, but it is so important for us to understand that we are never fully arrived: We never make it to a level of development where we never look back. It is imperative for us to understand that all of us, every single one of us, at many times and for the rest of our lives, will find ourselves floating through these stages. Our responses to relationships, personal feelings, and social movements will cause us to constantly float through these stages, and that is a fundamental part of being human. At no point in our journey here on earth do we arrive at a point of development or evolution and stay there forever. This racial identity development model gives us insight and helps us understand a reality that exists in every corner of our lives: gender, sexuality, relationship, grief, motivation, religion.

Every corner of human experience is fluid and moving and changing. We never graduate from grief; we never settle on identity. We are constantly being moved by the world and people around us, and ultimately, I think that is a beautiful and good thing—and it's a lot easier when you know it's happening. My most intellectual and nonreligious friends call me to ask for prayer when tragedy touches their lives. Why? Because that life experience causes them to float to another type of identity, and while day to day they may not believe there is a God who can help them in any way, when tragedy hits, they float right back to a place in their life when that reality was true, when they did believe in a God that could help them. Neither one of those realities is right or wrong, but do you see how fluid, how amorphous, our identity can be? How quickly it moves and bends to the experiences we are having here on this earth?

Now, in theory, I am sure we can relatively easily understand this. On paper it makes sense: Identity is not linear, humans are essentially giant walking and talking responses to their environments, and try as we might, we cannot always will ourselves to evolve, and that's fine. But what do we do when the people around us floating through their own identities collide with our floating? What do we do when we have friends whom we love and do life with, and then a situation in our lives throws us to opposite ends of our identity spectrums? What if my white friends start to feel as if now they are the ones being oppressed and I'm in my anger stage? What then?

Yes, in theory, people are allowed to float and respond to the situation around them, but what happens when they float to an ideology that allows them to believe that queer people are a threat, that our trans siblings are a threat? Am I supposed to have empathy for white supremacists cradling their guns in their arms like newborn babies? Am I supposed to support comedians opening anti-woke comedy clubs? And what do we do with the people we love who plant their feet in the sand and refuse to let the dissonance of life move them forward?

Theory is one thing, but the real harm we experience as people is another.

The reason I appreciate the racial identity model that we just went through so much is that it gives me a framework for myself that I am able to overlay on others in my life as well. The lived experience of the fluidity of my own identity reminds me how fragile everyone else's is too, and with that, it helps me understand not only how important boundaries are but also how they can shift with my life and the people around me.

I used to believe that boundaries were something that you set and that's it; you walk away, and that is the boundary forever. But that couldn't be further from how I understand boundaries today. The boundaries that I create, enact, and then ultimately reevaluate have to be aligned with my understanding of not only where I find my identity but also where the people around me find themselves. Boundaries are not something I sit down and set for my year on January 1; they are a nearly constant check-in with myself. And guess what? They change as much as I do. For most of my life, if you had asked me, "Would you ever stop talking to a friend because they voted differently from you?" I would have thought that sounded ridiculous. But during our last election in 2020? Every part of my identity was in defense mode, and I drew a hard line. I had a boundary as stiff as a board, and if you were a person who voted differently from me? That was it: blocked. I absolutely stopped talking to anyone who voted differently from me, because that was the boundary I needed; that was the boundary that held the container where my identity development was. But I'm not there anymore. I have floated to a space now where I feel more room, more space, and that boundary has shifted with me.

I have a friend, another Black woman who, through a series of situations in her own life, has been thrown back into the dissonance stage. She is angry—rightfully so—and she is working through that, and as someone who is not currently in the same space she is, I need to make sure I understand that is where she is. Our conversations are going to look different, and with that information, I can respond accordingly.

I am a person with so many identities, which are constantly shifting and moving and growing and evolving. I am a woman, a woman of color, a queer woman, a person of faith, a wife, a best friend, a co-worker, a daughter, a sister, a niece, a cousin, an author, a speaker, sometimes a runner. At any given point in my life, based on approximately one thousand factors, any one of those identities can take the front seat, can float to a different place. I didn't spend a lot of time on a regular basis thinking about what it meant to be a daughter until my parents got a late-in-life surprise divorce and that became the identity I spent days agonizing over: What did it mean to be a daughter? How would that label change as my family changed? Now I am sitting here writing this book, and my identity as an author has so much energy behind it, it is front and center and bringing with it joy and hope and truckloads of insecurity. Because I know that's what is happening, I am setting boundaries in my life and acting accordingly. That is how human interaction works—we take the information we know about ourselves and about other people, and we act accordingly. My sweet wife knows that writing makes me feel weird. I am far more tender than usual, my inner saboteur is always breathing down my neck, and so when I am in a season of writing, she hides little love notes and encouraging words in every corner of my things. I am looking at one now that she snuck onto my laptop. She tucked tiny notes into the case of my AirPods and under the cover of my iPad—and I am just now realizing that I have too many Apple products, but you get the idea: Our relationship shifts based on the way our identities are floating. That may make more sense in a romantic relationship, but it's also true about how we interact with the greater world around us too.

This framework and this understanding don't change my desire and commitment to fighting harm, resisting violence, and dismantling corrupt systems, but they do allow me to keep a certain amount of freedom and gray space for myself, knowing that the work won't look the same in every season. It's OK to rest, it's OK to be angry, it's OK to march in the streets, it's OK to get into good and hard conversations, and it's OK to let my phone go to voicemail. Listen, there is absolutely no complete and ever-true rule book for any of this, and my fear is that we have bought into the idea, and we have chosen external authorities who have made it seem that there is one statement, treatise, or creed that we can buy into or support that will always be true for us. That's madness.

A tweet that changes your life today could make you cringe tomorrow. You may read this book and hate it, and you may read it again in three months and like it (although if you hated it, I can't imagine you would pick it up again in three months, but you get the point). We have got to get past the idea that we are going to arrive at a point and stop moving, that we are going to finally set all the right boundaries with our family and move on, that we finally have the exact right group of friends, we have the right therapist, the right ideology, we read the right books and act in all the right ways—that we think the right things and we are set.

I hate to break it to you, but not only is that unrealistic, it's not healthy, either. All of it, all of us, all of who we are, shifts and moves as the winds of our life shift and move, and if you aren't willing to move with them, then you are missing so much of what there is here for us. If you are afraid to shift and move because you don't want the perception of you to change, then you are under the same spell as the people you probably hate.

We have got to get out from under the idea that we can arrive; we have to be willing to make the boundaries and do the work that is in front of us today, right now, this moment, and when it changes, we change with it. The work never stops, but our approach to the work should change as we do. Move your feet, friends; stay awake, do what is best for you now, and give yourself the freedom to float. It is going to happen anyway, so why spend your time fighting it? Maybe you aren't as radical as you were last year. Maybe you are more radical than ever, or maybe you had a baby, moved, changed jobs. Maybe someone you love is sick, maybe you quit your job, went through a breakup, left a religion, found a new religion, fought with a racist family member, realized you are the racist family member, heard a joke that hurt your feelings, made a joke that hurt feelings. All of it, literally all of it, is happening all the time, and every moment it changes our approach if we let it. Stop looking for the right answers and try to just take the next right step instead.

8

Charting a Way Forward

THE WORLD IS CHANGING AT A RATE MOST LIVING HUMANS are unfamiliar with, and we are changing with it. We are connected to one another in ways that we could have never imagined, and we are learning that connection doesn't always bring out the best in us—or the worst. There's so much nuance to be experienced in the change that has become even more inevitable to us. Any rule book we could try to write or creed we could try to come up with will very shortly find itself antiquated on the other side of a new reality, and personally, I love that. I don't think we are ever meant to feel as if we have arrived, as if we have the answer, but the best we can do is feel as though we are fully here, engaged, and living in the present moment and all that it brings. New information, changes in relationships, new ideas. Can we stay tuned to ourselves and the world around us as both are rapidly expanding?

I love tattoos. I've lost count of how many I have, but it's got to be somewhere between ten and twenty with the constant hope and desire for more. I love getting a tattoo to commemorate a moment or idea or thought I had that I felt changed me, shaped me, or gave me a new lens through which I could more clearly see this life and the important things in it. One of my favorite tattoos is one that my wife and I got together. We both have the words *Stay Awake* inked permanently on our arms. One of the things that we both fear most is the reality that we could go numb, that we could stop paying attention, that we could look up one day and say, "Where have the last ten years gone?" We just don't want to miss anything; we want to be present in our life, the hard parts, the good parts—we want to be awake for all of it. We don't want to fall asleep, find ourselves on autopilot, and miss all of the juicy goodness that exists for us every day. Now, just to be clear, we don't always nail this. Sometimes on hour three of mindlessly scrolling TikTok, I look at that tattoo and I'm like, "Maybe later," but at my best I am present, able to hold the nuance, and feel that I am a part of a way forward. In those moments, I have found that there are three steps that help me get there.

I did not intend for this to be a story about my tattoos, but it's worth noting that the first step I like to take in my quest to be present and awake in life is to remember—and yes, I do also have a tattoo that says *Remember*, but that's beside the point. I think too often we can get so wrapped up in our reality and in our time that we forget about all of the life and humanity and experience that existed before now. In the past five years, I have heard many different people on different platforms say something to the effect of "This is the most divided America has ever been." Have you heard this sentiment? Like, did y'all forget about the Civil War? Slavery? Internment camps? I'm not saying America is currently thriving at her best, but it would feel silly to imagine that this is the most divided we have ever been. The reason it's important to remember times of division before this, or to remember people before us, is because there is just so much to learn from them, from their experience, from their time here. If we cut ourselves off from thinking anyone knows what it is like to be us, then we miss out on massive amounts of wisdom. If you want to be present in this reality, you have to be willing to get some perspective and wisdom from the ones before us. Remembering is an absolutely fundamental part of grounding us in this present moment.

I know we talked about progressive amnesia earlier, and while I am a person who tries to love herself well most days, I am also deeply connected to and remember clearly the versions of me that have made mistakes. When I was working at a megachurch, one thing about my boss that bothered me (aside from his secret homophobia and sexism, of course) was the fact that when he would preach onstage, every example that he used from his own life was a story or experience in which he was the hero. He would tell some story about how good he was at being a dad and then say something like, "You see how much I love my kids? Can you believe God loves you even more than that?" It always bothered me because, yes, I do think it's important to give yourself a pat on the back and recognize how far you've come and the good you do in the world, but the connection to our flawed humanity is, in my opinion, just as important. It's what allows us to empathize with other people in the world. It's what gives us room to understand. It reminds us that though we have made mistakes, we can still keep growing, and every time that happens we rewire our brains to get ready for the next time.

One thing that was important to me as I set out to write this book was that I only wanted to tell stories about myself when I didn't get it, when I missed the mark, when I made mistakes. Yes, part of that I'm sure is a response to being traumatized from having to listen to a grown man brag about himself every Sunday for years, but I also think it's important. Remembering myself as a person who has had both success and failure allows me to stay present in it all when it comes my way. Remembering that I have fallen victim to harmful ideology and found my way out is not something I feel ashamed about; it's something I feel proud of, and it's also something that I know is possible because I experienced it. I am a real person, not a hero, not a villain, not a monolith, and staying close to all of the memories that make up who I am is one of the most important parts of my work. I remember all of the times before I knew what I know now, and that remembrance has no option but to keep me even more grounded in this present moment, knowing that one day, I will likely look back on who I am now with the same compassion.

The second step that helps me stay awake and present in this current moment is imagination. One of my heroes in this life is Octavia Butler. Octavia Butler saw the world as it was and wrote about what it could be. For better, for worse, in all imaginable ways, she was able to write and bring us into her imagination—an imagination that was ignited from this reality. She used her imagination to help us understand complex and nuanced human ideas in a way that included both fantasy and horror and allowed our brains to expand and wrap themselves around problems like racism, climate change, and patriarchy, and she did this all by bringing us into her imagination. By telling these stories in a way we had never heard them. I have hung my hat on many things that she said, but one thing that truly changed the way I approached this life was when she showed us that all justice work is fiction writing. She explained that anytime you are trying to imagine a world that does not yet exist, you are writing fiction. Isn't that incredible? Think about it: When Martin Luther King, Jr., said "I have a dream," and went on to explain how he saw little Black kids and white kids playing on a playground together, that was him bringing us into his imagination—that was fiction writing. He was imagining a world that wasn't real, that didn't exist.

As much as the writers of *Game of Thrones* are writing fiction and imagining a world where dragons fly around and ravens send messages to people, I too am creating a new world when I sit and imagine and hope and describe what the world would be like without guns. A world without guns is one of my deepest fantasies; it's the world that I imagine, the fantasy I have written in my head. The fictional narrative I see is of a world where kids go to school without fear, where conflict resolution is passed around like candy at a parade to all who want it. I have built out this fantasy and I dream about it, and it consumes me sometimes. The fantasy of it all feels intoxicating—it's one of my favorite places for my mind to go when it wanders. This experience of imagination is not unique or specific to me. We have all followed or benefitted from people who have let their minds and imaginations wander, people whose minds floated to a world that didn't exist yet, so they created it. We live in the world we live in because people before us imagined it and made it a reality. Imagination is one of our most sacred practices as people.

The difference between justice work as fiction and just plain fiction writing is that one draws us to action. When Stan Lee created the Marvel Universe, that imagination was for imagination's sake: What if the god of thunder came down to earth and fell in love? What if he comically made friends with a talking raccoon from space? What if together, they helped the Hulk escape from a garbage planet where Jeff Goldblum was the leader? This is imagination and it's fun and wonderful and I've seen every Marvel movie that exists, but it is not necessarily the type of imagination that calls us to action. Imagining that there is a god from Asgard who flies with a hammer is fun but does not require anything of us. But imagining that queer folks all over the world have access to the basic rights and safety that they deserve is the kind of imagination we need to practice. It is the kind that haunts us toward action.

In 2022, my wife and I had the opportunity to go to a film festival in Telluride, Colorado. The first night of the festival, the very first film we saw had me in tears and in awe. The film is called *Of Medicine and Miracles* and is the story of how the immunologist Carl June figured out how to train T cells to fight cancer. If you, like me, have no idea what that means, then allow me to, with some mediocrity, explain. Essentially Dr. June had a series of life experiences that set him up to have an imagination for something that didn't exist yet; his career in medicine had taken multiple turns caused by cultural and global changes. In the 1990s, Dr. June started to focus on patients who were HIV positive and patients with AIDS, which at the time was not a demographic many were working with. Dr. June started to zero in on specifically studying T cells in those patients—and now here's where my description of what happens next probably has some significant biological plot holes, but please feel free to watch the movie. Essentially, Dr. June became obsessed with how T cells in these patients seemed as if they were being rewired or retrained in a way, and years later, when his career turned its gaze toward fighting cancer, he took that T cell obsession with him and had this thought: If T cells can be rewired by HIV, could I rewire them to fight cancer? And just so you know, that is a mind-blowing imaginative idea and, up until that point, had been nonexistent. No one had ever trained T cells or thought about training

T cells. There were no so-called living treatments for cancer yet, and he imagined a world where you could take T cells out of someone's body, train them to fight their specific type of cancer, and then put them back in their body, and that imagination, that fictional narrative he was writing, haunted and obsessed him and drove him to action. It took him quite a while, but eventually he did it. The movie focuses on how his living T cell treatment saved the life of a little girl named Emily who had recieved a terminal leukemia diagnosis at six years old. It was moving and tearjerking, and for the rest of the weekend anytime I saw that man walking down the street, I reacted as if he were George Clooney.

My wife and I sat having drinks after the screening, still marveling at what we had seen and remembering the reality that every amazing thing we know or experience or see came from someone's imagination—imagination that drove them to action. Imagination is not just for fantasy and escape—imagination is a sacred part of how we evolve as people. An imagination for a world where women vote, an imagination for how we fight cancer differently, an imagination for how we heal the planet, an imagination for a world without guns. Imagination is how we move the world forward. But the third and final step to being present in our life after we remember, after we imagine, is this: We have to be ready to act. We have to act, and we also have to be willing to release the results of our actions.

I think what can be difficult for a lot of us is to act without knowing whether or not it will work. To act without knowing if it's the "right" way to do something. Those questions stop a lot of us from acting at all. We let a lot of things stop us from acting—we have inner critics and outer critics, we lack hope or belief that change is possible, we feel too small, or our problems feel too big—and I think so much of our work lies in our ability to act in spite of those realities.

I am married to a creative, and if you are a creative or love a creative, you may deeply know and understand the reality that literally no project is ever done or ready or complete. My wife would work on a design project for eight years if she could. She would move and adjust and change because it's never perfectly up to her standards; it could always be better. Many years ago I was at a conference, and I heard an executive from Pixar talk about how their whole team has to agree to just release a project when they feel they are eighty percent done with it, because they all know they will never feel one hundred percent. Isn't it wild that *Toy Story 3* is someone's eighty percent effort? *Up* is eighty percent! But this isn't just a concept for creatives. I know all of us understand what it feels like not to do something: not to share a story, take a class, write a book, apply for a job, email a congressperson, have a hard conversation with a partner or family member. There are hundreds of things that we decide not to do because we are afraid we don't know the exact right way to do them, and we are probably right. Exact perfection isn't the goal; mistakes are inevitable, change is slow, but inaction is regrettable. And by the way, there is no rule book, no standards, no "Here's the exact right way to do everything, and if you mess up, this book will be thrown at you." I know the internet may make it seem as if that is actually true, but it's not. You have to be willing to act based on who you are (and remember, that identity is always floating), where you are, what resources you have, and what you see in your imagination. Release the project at eighty percent; we need you to.

One of my favorite periods of history to study is the American civil rights movement. It is the period from about 1954 to 1968, when we saw the greatest movement, the greatest leaders, and some of the most unifying and defining moments in our history. One of my favorite things about this movement is how many people played wildly different roles all in pursuit of the same goal. For around five years of my life, I led these trips called civil rights tours. I would pack people in a van, and we would track some of the routes of the Freedom Riders. We would interview people in every city, visit museums and historic sites, and just deep dive into the nuance and details of this time.

One of the things that continues to blow my mind is how truly vast this movement was. Maybe you know about the Freedom Riders or the March on Washington or the Black Panther Party, but there were thousands and thousands of people, doing what they felt was right from their vantage point, their imagination, their inspiration, and it took all of them, literally everyone, to make this movement move. There were people in Montgomery who had cars, and during the bus boycott they became block leaders for their neighborhoods and drove to the store and pharmacy to make sure everyone on their street had everything they needed and could survive without needing to get on the bus. There were college students who were doing sit-ins at restaurants, getting arrested every weekend, organizing nonviolent protest after nonviolent protest. There were older folks feeding the college students, making sure they had places to stay in each town. There were folks printing and making signs for the protests; there were folks marching; there were Black business owners making space for folks to just come and rest at their café or have fun at their nightclub. There were people in politics working, in the streets having conversations, and in the rural areas registering people to vote. There were tutors to help people pass the polling tests; there were teams supporting the big leaders whose names we know; there were families supporting the leaders you've probably never heard of; there were churches holding space, there were artists creating anthems—and all of it was needed. All of it was valid; all of it was necessary.

You cannot look at a movement like that and ask, "What was the right way to respond? What was the most helpful approach?" No, you look at a movement like that and let it be a reminder that your job is to take your imagination, your resources, your position in life, and act as only you can. We really need to stop trying to have our action be the most socially acceptable approach, and we need to start understanding that we are a part of a bigger movement. Your role is not going to look the same as the next person's in your newsfeed, and if it does, I would suggest you dig deeper. Stop standing still because you don't know whether or not everyone will agree with your action, or you don't know if it's the right action to take. We need people who act. Release the project at eighty percent; do what you can. Anything else is a lie, and anything less is a miss.

Let me give you an example. I am a person of color who grew up in predominantly white schools and churches for literally all of my life. It wasn't until college that I had a friend group that was majority other Black women, and mostly not for any reason other than there weren't enough around me before that. There were three other Black girls in my high school grade, and I was friends with all of them, but I went to a very large high school and that is a very sad statistic. In college, I got very involved in the Black student group on campus—I eventually became the president my senior year. I was on the step team despite having questionable amounts of rhythm, and even though I was still at a predominantly white school, I found spaces and moments that allowed me to feel the feeling that only being in those rooms could provide. I learned the deep breath that you let out in those spaces; I learned so much about myself and became even more settled in my identity.

I still exist as a person who holds both of those experiences. I know what it feels like to be around Black women and the deep breath and exhale of those environments. I am also married to a white woman and have lots of white friends, and my life still exists in both spaces. Because of that—because of how I grew up and who my family is—I have become very comfortable and confident having conversations about race and racism with white people. Why?

Because my life has set me up for it. Now, here is the nuance that we often miss: Our experiences are not meant to be universal, so when I hear messages that say, "It is not people of color's job to teach you," I think that is absolutely true. Black people are not required to teach white people. But I personally enjoy it. I do not represent all Black people. I do not think all Black people need to or even should feel the same way as me, but when I look at my history and my experience and my current life, that is a way for me to engage in the work; it's a path that makes sense for what I have and where I am. It would be outrageous for me to say, "This is the way I am doing it, so everyone needs to do it this way," and it would also be unreasonable for me to say, "There's someone who says this isn't their way, so I should stop."

Our life experiences are not universal, so stop trying to make them so. You cannot boil everything down to a tweet, and your work will not look exactly like your neighbor's. Maybe if we spent a little less time critiquing and more time moving, we could create some beautiful change in a world that so desperately needs it. My way is not the right way; it's just right for me, and also, it may change, and that's OK too. All I know is that I can't and won't do nothing. Everyone doesn't have to agree with me, act like me, think like me, or move like me, but I do believe that other people and I are working toward the same goal, and it will take all of us doing what we can from where we are to get there.

It takes thousands of people working from all angles to make a movement move. If you get caught up in the critique and stop moving every time someone (probably on the internet) has a different vantage point, then I question your ability to get very far. Go with what you know, learn along the way, adapt to new information, but please do not let all of the outside noise keep you from acting on that sacred and holy imagination you have running through your mind. It will not be perfect; I guarantee you will make mistakes, but that is the exact kind of human action we need right now.

I have heard it said that our job here on this earth is to plant seeds for trees that we will never sit under. We remember, we imagine, we act, and beyond that we trust that the seeds we have planted, the sprouts we have watered, and the trees we have trimmed will remain long beyond our time here. We have to be able to turn our gaze beyond the present moment; we have to remind ourselves that we are a part of something bigger, something greater—something that requires us to move.

I want to end with another story from the faith tradition that I grew up in. It's not a story that I was ever told as a kid, and even through six years at a Christian school, I still never heard it. It's a small story that you only notice if you are paying attention. It's a small note inside a much larger moment, and it has become one of my favorite stories in the whole Bible. OK, here's the story. There was a man named Joseph—the jury is still out on whether he did in fact own an amazing Technicolor dreamcoat, but he was an Israelite sold into slavery in Egypt by his brothers. He then, through a series of events, worked his way up to

be the right-hand man of Pharaoh—the leader in Egypt—
and saved his family from death by famine. Years later, seeing all that he had seen in his life—his own journey from
enslavement to leadership—and perhaps knowing that all
of his people would eventually become enslaved in Egypt as
well . . . he still believed that freedom would come for them.
On his deathbed, as his time was coming to an end, he
made a request—he said that he knew the Israelites would
one day find freedom, and when they did, he asked that his
bones be taken with them and buried in the land of the free.

OK, so just to recap, there is a man who was sold into
slavery, who lived his life in service to a man who was not
deserving of the power he had acquired. He saw the odds
and still did what he could in his time, knowing that he
would not live to see freedom for his people—but he knew
that the day would come and asked that his bones be taken
with them when it did. Isn't that wild? Well, around four
hundred years later (as the story is told), the Israelites did
find freedom, as Moses led them out of Egypt. There is a
small note in that story that says, on their way out of Egypt,
on their way to freedom, Moses was carrying Joseph's
bones with him. Joseph was buried in the land of freedom.

I think of that story every time I feel overwhelmed with
the world around me and how big every problem feels, how
much change I feel we need. The story makes me aware of
two things: I am carrying with me the bones of the people
who came before me, and those people believed in the freedom I now live in. They believed with everything in them
that freedom would come, though they might not live to see

it. It's their bones that I carry with me. When my wife and I casually walked into the office to pick up our marriage certificate, we were carrying people with us. When I, a queer Black woman, got the contract to write this book, I was carrying bones with me. The life that I live is built on those who acted, who kept hope and imagination for a world they would never see, and now I do the same. I hope my bones find their way to a world I believe in, hope for, imagine, and act toward, but know I will not see.

Listen, we live in a world that has experienced a lot of change, and we need a lot more change still, but please do not fool yourself into thinking this moment right now is the only one that matters. There is a lot of work to do: We need to eradicate white supremacy, we need the guns to go, we need to heal the planet, we need Black trans folks to live long lives, we need foster youth to be set up for success, we probably don't need to colonize Mars, we need housing for everyone, and we need healthcare that is accessible to all. We have so much to do, and I will work toward the change knowing that I may see some of it in my life, and my bones may be carried through the rest of it, and I am OK with that. I sit under trees people planted for me, and I will throw seeds out for the rest of my life; maybe I will see the leaves and maybe I won't, but if we want to see any of this change happen, we have got to get some perspective. Remember whose bones you are carrying with you; imagine the world you want to see and go act on it. And no, it is not going to be perfect, it is not going to be easy, you will make mistakes, there will be hard times, there will be pain and grief and loss and joy, but we need people who are willing to hold both, to keep moving.

We have to be deeply committed to navigating the nuance that exists when we disagree with the ones we love—our grandparents and parents and partners, our friends and cousins. We must be willing to do the work that allows us to stay in relationships. We must draw and redraw boundaries, share stories and experiences, and ultimately find what I think most of us are looking for: a way to disagree with someone and still hold them close. And for goodness' sake, if we are going to see the change in this world that we so desperately need, we have got to stop arguing with strangers on the internet.

Do your work, act on your own sacred imagination, hope that you see some of the change, and believe that your bones will see the fullness of it one day.

ACKNOWLEDGMENTS

To my wonderful wife, Sami: Thank you for constantly being the mirror I need to truly see myself. It is an honor to evolve with you.

To JM: This book would not be here without you. Thank you for believing in it and in me.

To New Abbey: Thank you for being a place where ideas can turn into words and words into action.

This book came to life with endless love and support from my family, friends, and community. I will be forever grateful for all of you.

ABOUT THE AUTHOR

BRIT BARRON is a renowned speaker, teacher, storyteller, and author of *Worth It: Overcome Your Fears and Embrace the Life You Were Made For*. Brit's ideas and accomplishments have garnered the attention of numerous prominent national publications, making her a highly sought-after speaker on the topics of sexuality, spirituality, race, storytelling, and personal development. Brit and her wife, Sami, live in Los Angeles, California, with their dog Charles Barkley and numerous houseplants that they do their best to keep alive.

britbarron.com
Facebook: britbarronofficial
Instagram: @britbarron
X: @britbarronco

Also available from
Brit Barron

The *Do You Still Talk to Grandma? Workbook* is an essential guide for the concrete actions we can take toward transformative justice in our everyday lives.

CONVERGENT